**SOUTH-WESTERN
EDUCATIONAL PUBLISHING**

STUDENT ACTIVITIES GUIDE

# Business Principles and Management

TENTH EDITION

BY

KENNETH E. EVERARD
*Professor of Management, Trenton State College*
*Trenton, New Jersey*

JAMES L. BURROW
*Associate Professor, North Carolina State University*
*Raleigh, North Carolina*

I(T)P
International Thomson Publishing

South-Western Educational Publishing is a division of International Thomson Publishing, Inc. The ITP trademark is used under license.


ISBN: 0-538-62468-X
11 12 G 03 02
Printed in the United States of America
Cover design by Lamson Design, Cincinnati

# CONTENTS

# PREFACE TO WORKBOOK

A variety of activities appear in this workbook to help you learn the material you have studied in the Tenth Edition of *Business Principles and Management*. Follow your teacher's instructions as you select workbook activities to complete. After completing your assigned tasks, you should have an excellent understanding of the principles that appear in the textbook. Four types of exercises are provided: Study Guides, Controversial Issues, Problems, and a Continuing Project.

The Study Guide activities allow you to check your understanding of basic facts by involving you in answering yes-no, multiple choice, and matching or fill-in questions for each chapter. The Controversial Issues exercises challenge you to look at two questions that may be answered "yes" or "no." After studying each issue, you should provide reasons to support your answers. The Problems section requires you to study and solve realistic business problems and, in some situations, to perform calculations to arrive at sound decisions.

The Continuing Project is the last activity in each chapter. This project will likely provide you with one of the most valuable ways to learn about business because you will be learning how to start and operate a new enterprise. After finishing each chapter, you will be asked several types of critical questions that will affect this new business. The same business is used throughout the Continuing Project so that you will experience what it is like to become an entrepreneur.

Each of the four types of activities—Study Guides, Controversial Issues, Problems, and Continuing Project—will provide you with a different way to review and learn the textbook material. Enjoy working through the exercises assigned by your teacher as you acquire new business knowledge by applying critical-thinking skills.

Kenneth E. Everard
Jim Burrow

# Study Guide

**Part A**—*Directions:* Indicate your answer to each of the following questions by circling either yes or no in the Answers column.

| | | Answers | | For Scoring |
|---|---|---|---|---|
| 1. | Do more than 18 million businesses currently exist in the United States? ...... | yes | no | 1. _____ |
| 2. | Do businesses vary in size from one employee to more than a million employees? ................................................................................................... | yes | no | 2. _____ |
| 3. | Is an organization that produces or distributes a good or service for profit called a business? ................................................................................... | yes | no | 3. _____ |
| 4. | Do service firms produce goods? ................................................................. | yes | no | 4. _____ |
| 5. | Does marketing deal with money matters related to running a business? ....... | yes | no | 5. _____ |
| 6. | Does the supply of a product refer to the number of similar products that will be bought at a given time and at a given price? ......................................... | yes | no | 6. _____ |
| 7. | Do industrial businesses produce goods that other businesses use to make things? | yes | no | 7. _____ |
| 8. | Are banks and investment companies classified as industrial types of businesses? | yes | no | 8. _____ |
| 9. | Because a government provides fire and police protection, can it can be considered an industry? ................................................................................. | yes | no | 9. _____ |
| 10. | Are there about three times as many employees in production industries than in all other industries? ................................................................................. | yes | no | 10. _____ |
| 11. | Does effectiveness occur when an organization produces needed goods or services quickly at low cost? ............................................................................ | yes | no | 11. _____ |
| 12. | Are firms that are extremely efficient always very effective? ......................... | yes | no | 12. _____ |
| 13. | Is the concept of total quality management a commitment to excellence that is accomplished by teamwork and continual improvement? .............................. | yes | no | 13. _____ |
| 14. | Is the Malcolm Baldrige Award presented only to small companies? .............. | yes | no | 14. _____ |
| 15. | Does output refer to the quantity, or amount, produced within a given time? | yes | no | 15. _____ |
| 16. | Did productivity rates in the United States fall between 1985 and 1990? ...... | yes | no | 16. _____ |
| 17. | Has the United States been one of the world's leading contributors of new inventions? ...................................................................................................... | yes | no | 17. _____ |
| 18. | Did many small firms recently increase their workforce by adding more high-paying rather than low-paying jobs? ........................................................... | yes | no | 18. _____ |
| 19. | Is the franchisor the distributor of a franchised product or service? ................ | yes | no | 19. _____ |
| 20. | Does risk in business involve competition from new products? ...................... | yes | no | 20. _____ |

**Part B**—*Directions:* For each of the following statements, select the word, or group of words, that best completes the statement. In the Answers column, write the letter corresponding to the answer selected.

| | Answers | For Scoring |
|---|---|---|

1. The business activity that is involved with how goods or services are exchanged between producers and consumers is (a) production, (b) marketing, (c) finance, (d) manufacturing. ................................................................ _____ 1. _____

2. Which is an example of a commercial business firm? (a) mining, (b) construction, (c) banking, (d) manufacturing. ................................................ _____ 2. _____

3. Which type of business firm has the largest number of employees? (a) wholesale and retail trade, (b) government (c) manufacturing, (d) general services. ........ _____ 3. _____

4. Which type of business firm had the greatest increase in number from 1975 to 1989? (a) manufacturing, (b) wholesale trade, (c) retail trade, (d) services. ..... _____ 4. _____

5. Which of the following refers to the concept that is dedicated to the commitment of excellence? (a) ESOP, (b) TQM, (c) GDP, (d) T&I. ........................... _____ 5. _____

6. The main reason the productivity of factory workers increased for many years was that businesses were using (a) fewer workers, (b) new or improved equipment, (c) lower-paid workers, (d) more part-time workers. ............................. _____ 6. _____

7. Which nation had the most productive workers in 1990? (a) United States, (b) Canada, (c) Japan, (d) England. ................................................................ _____ 7. _____

8. What effect does advanced technology usually have on the cost of each item produced by a business? (a) cost stays about the same, (b) cost increases, (c) cost decreases, (d) revenue and cost break even. ................................................ _____ 8. _____

9. Approximately what percent of the GDP comes from revenue that is generated from all small businesses? (a) 20%, (b) 30%, (c) 40%, (d) 50%. .................... _____ 9. _____

10. In the typical franchise business, the franchisee does NOT receive (a) help in selecting a location for the business, (b) special training in how to operate efficiently, (c) guaranteed profit, (d) exclusive rights to sell in a specified geographic area. ...................................................................................... _____ 10. _____

11. Which of the following best describes risk? (a) insurance, (b) possibility of failure, (c) net losses a business suffers, (d) protection. .................................... _____ 11. _____

12. Approximately what percent of all business firms cease operations within six to seven years of startup? (a) 10%, (b) 20%, (c) 35%, (d) 50%. ......................... _____ 12. _____

13. The two primary reasons for business failures are (a) inadequate planning and experience, (b) overexpansion and neglect, (c) economic and finance causes, (d) disaster and fraud. ...................................................................................... _____ 13. _____

14. An employee who is given funds and freedom to create a special unit or department within a company in order to develop a new product, process, or service is called an (a) apprentice, (b) entrepreneur, (c) intrapreneur (d) investor. .......... _____ 14. _____

15. What occurs when an organization produces needed goods or services quickly? (a) total quality management, (b) effectiveness, (c), efficiency, (d) productivity. _____ 15. _____

**Directions:** Study each controversial issue carefully. Follow the advice of your teacher before listing in the columns provided reasons why people might answer Yes or No. Your teacher may want you to work with a classmate, talk with others in your community to gather information, or use the library to gather facts.

1-1. In order to protect U.S. businesses from foreign competitors, should the federal government provide financial aid that would enable troubled businesses to survive?

| Reasons for "Yes" | Reasons for "No" |
| --- | --- |
| | |

1-2. Because the failure rate among new businesses is high, should potential entrepreneurs be required to pass a test on how to run a business?

| Reasons for "Yes" | Reasons for "No" |
| --- | --- |
| | |

# PROBLEMS

**1-A.** Check the column that correctly classifies whether each business listed below is an industrial business or a commercial business.

|  | | Commercial | Industrial |
|---|---|---|---|
| 1. | Crushed stone mill ........................................................................ | _____ | _____ |
| 2. | Credit card business ..................................................................... | _____ | _____ |
| 3. | Sporting goods shop ...................................................................... | _____ | _____ |
| 4. | Home building firm........................................................................ | _____ | _____ |
| 5. | Health care center ......................................................................... | _____ | _____ |

**1-B.** For each of the activities listed below, check the column that indicates whether the activity applies primarily to effectiveness or efficiency. Assume your company operates a lawn-mowing service and must compete with four other companies.

|  | | Effectiveness | Efficiency |
|---|---|---|---|
| 1. | Ask customers what they like most and least about your service. ................... | _____ | _____ |
| 2. | Buy new equipment to prevent lost mowing time from breakdowns. ............ | _____ | _____ |
| 3. | Mow all lawns located near each other on the same day. .............................. | _____ | _____ |
| 4. | Add new services such as fertilizing and watering lawns. ............................ | _____ | _____ |
| 5. | Lower your operating costs by buying gas in quantity at lower prices. ........... | _____ | _____ |
| 6. | Sharpen blades more often to improve appearance of grass. .......................... | _____ | _____ |
| 7. | Train your workers in customer courtesy. ...................................................... | _____ | _____ |

**1-C.** The wealth of a nation can be shown in the percentage of households owning selected electronic appliances. From the information shown below in percents, answer the questions provided.

| Appliance | U.S. | Denmark | Germany | France | Spain |
|---|---|---|---|---|---|
| Microwave | 61 | 14 | 36 | 25 | 9 |
| Dishwasher | 43 | 26 | 34 | 33 | 11 |
| Television | 93* | 98 | 97 | 94 | 98 |
| Clothes dryer | 51 | 22 | 17 | 12 | 5 |

*Color televisions only
*Source: Statistical Abstract of the United States, 1992*

1. Based on the electrical appliances owned, in which country is the standard of living the high-

   est?_____ the lowest?_____

2. Which country has the second-best standard of living? _____

3. Which electrical appliance is the most popular among all five countries? _____

4. Study the information above and the information shown in Fig. 1-5 in your textbook. Provide a reason why

   there are fewer televisions in U.S. households than in the households of other countries.

   _____

   _____

   _____

**1-D.** Place a check in the column that shows the form of business ownership that best identifies the situation of a firm with 100 employees.

| | Employee Stock Ownership Plan | Entrepreneur | Intrapreneur |
|---|:---:|:---:|:---:|
| 1. Each year all 100 workers buy 20 ownership shares of the firm. ........................................ | _____ | _____ | _____ |
| 2. One of these workers sells all her shares to the remaining workers in order to start a business of her own. ........................................ | _____ | _____ | _____ |
| 3. Three of the workers agree to work separately from the others to create new processes for increasing output and improving quality. ........................................ | _____ | _____ | _____ |
| 4. Two workers quit to form their own business making a special product they have agreed to sell to their old firm. ........................................ | _____ | _____ | _____ |

**1-E.** Are you the kind of person who could start a business and make it go? Here is a way to find out. For each question below, check the answer that says what you feel or comes closest to it. Be honest with yourself.

1.    *Are you a self-starter?*
____    I do things on my own. Nobody must tell me to get going.
____    If someone gets me started, I keep going all right.
____    Easy does it. I do not put myself out until I have to.

2.    *How do you feel about other people?*
____    I like people. I can get along with just about anybody.
____    I have plenty of friends—I do not need anyone else.
____    Most people irritate me.

3.    *Can you lead others?*
____    I can get most people to follow when I start something.
____    I can give the orders if someone tells me what we should do.
____    I let someone else get things moving. Then I go along if I feel like it.

4.    *Can you take responsibility?*
____    I like to take charge of things and see them through.
____    I will take over if I have to, but I would rather let someone else be responsible.
____    There are always some "eager beavers" around wanting to show how smart they are. I say let them be responsible.

5.    *How good an organizer are you?*
____    I like to have a plan before I start. I am usually the one to get things lined up when the group wants to do something.
____    I do all right unless things get too confused. Then I quit.
____    I get all set and then something comes along and presents too many problems. So I just take things as they come.

6.    *How good a worker are you?*
____    I can keep going as long as I need to. I do not mind working hard for something I want.
____    I will work hard for a while, but when I have had enough, that's it.
____    I do not believe that hard work gets you anywhere.

7.    *Can you make decisions?*
____    I can make up my mind in a hurry if I have to. It usually turns out okay, too.
____    I can make decisions if I have plenty of time. If I have to make up my mind quickly, I think later I should have decided the other way.
____    I do not like to be the one who has to decide things.

5

8.    *Can people trust what you say?*
____    You bet they can. I do not say things I do not mean.
____    I try to be honest most of the time, but sometimes I just say what is easiest.
____    Why bother if the other person does not know the difference?

9.    *Can you stick with it?*
____    If I make up my mind to do something, I do not let anything stop me.
____    I usually finish what I start—if it goes well.
____    If it does not go right at the start, I quit. Why beat your brains out?

10.    *How good is your health?*
____    I never run down!
____    I have enough energy for most things I want to do.
____    I run out of energy sooner than most of my friends seem to.


Count the checks you made. They should add to 10.

How many checks are there beside the first answer to each question? _____

How many checks are there beside the second answer to each question? _____

How many checks are there beside the third answer to each question? _____


If most of your checks are beside the first answers, you probably have what it takes to run a business. If not, you are likely to have more trouble than you can handle by yourself. Better find a partner who is strong where you are weak. If many checks are beside the third answer, you should not consider going into business for yourself. You will be better off working for someone else as an employee.


1-F. Many newly opened active businesses are started each year. Study the information given for a year. Then answer the questions below.

| No. of Employees | No. of Firms | Percent of Firms |
|---|---|---|
| 2 or fewer | 135,010 | _____ |
| 3 to 5 | 53,230 | _____ |
| 6 to 10 | 24,902 | _____ |
| 11 to 20 | 11,204 | _____ |
| 21 or more | 9,364 | _____ |
| Totals | _____ | _____ |

1.  How many businesses were started during the year? Record your answer in the space provided above.
2.  For the number of employees in each category shown, what is the percent of new startups involved? Record your answers in the space provided above.
3.  What percent of the total businesses that start have fewer than six employees? _____
4.  Based upon the figures above and your answers to the questions asked, place a check on the line provided ONLY if the statement is correct.

   a.  The majority of newly started businesses have two or fewer employees. _____

   b.  Less than one percent of the newly started businesses have six or more employees. _____

   c.  Over eighty percent of the newly started businesses have five or fewer employees. _____

6

**1-G.** Ten years ago Raul and Sangita Patel started a small restaurant that sold mostly seafood. The high quality of the food, fair prices, and an attractive dining room caused the business to become very successful. Two years ago after the first restaurant was opened, they opened an identical restaurant for their oldest daughter to operate in a nearby community. This restaurant is also successful. Today the Patels have five restaurants, and each is doing well.

The Patels would like to continue opening restaurants in other nearby communities. However, they know they cannot operate any more restaurants because even now their time is much too limited. For that reason they have been thinking of other ways to expand their business. A friend, Jason Johnson, suggested that they start a franchise and he be given the first chance to operate one of the restaurants in a nearby state.

1. Do you think operating under a franchise arrangement will work for the Patels? Yes _____ No _____

2. If the Patels gave Jason Johnson the opportunity to open a restaurant under a franchise agreement, who would be the franchisor? _____

3. Who would be the franchisee? _____

4. List some of the kinds of help that the Patels might provide Jason Johnson under a franchise agreement.

   _____

5. How will the Patels benefit by franchising their restaurants to people such as Jason Johnson? _____

   _____

   _____

6. How can the Patels control the way others run their franchised restaurants? _____

   _____

   _____

# CONTINUING PROJECT

## Developing a New Business

This workbook has been developed to help you learn about business. The study of business can be particularly interesting if, while you are learning, you have the chance to apply what you learn. When you can use business principles in a project you select and design, they become very meaningful.

You may already be working in a business or expect to become an employee in the near future. As an employee, you have the opportunity to observe business practices and compare them to the information you are learning in this course. You can also ask questions of your co-workers, supervisor, and the owner or manager of the company.

It is possible that a member of your family or a close friend operates his/her own business. Increasingly new, small businesses are being started by students while still in high school or college. You or one of your classmates might already be a business owner or are considering starting a business. Those experiences or plans will make this course even more valuable.

This Continuing Project is designed to prepare you for a career in business, particularly if you are interested in business ownership or management. You will experience making many types of decisions faced by managers or a person starting a new business. You will see the type and amount of work and study needed to make effective decisions. You will learn how to apply the information you have learned as you study *Business Principles and Management.* The relationship between the various parts of business will become even clearer as you continue this project throughout the course.

## Project Organization

The Continuing Project is organized so that you can complete a part of the project as you finish each chapter. You will immediately be able to use what you have learned as you gather information and use it to make specific decisions about a new business.

Each chapter project contains two types of activities. In the Data Collection activities, you will be asked to collect information needed by managers to make decisions and solve problems. By completing the Data Collection activities, you will learn about the sources and types of business information available to decision makers. You will see that having appropriate information available aids in the decision-making process.

In the Analysis activities you are asked to answer questions and make specific decisions related to a new business. These activities show you the specific types of decisions that must be made by business owners and managers, how those decisions relate to each other, and how your developing knowledge and understanding of business improves your decision-making abilities. Your teacher will give you specific instructions about the activities you will complete.

## Project Overview

Fast food businesses have been popular and successful for many years. That success is based on the large number of people who eat many meals outside the home. Many of those people are willing to eat at restaurants offering a limited menu and very little service if the food is of high quality, is available quickly, and is at a relatively low price. Starting in the 1950s and 1960s, national fast food franchises were developed; many grew rapidly in response to changing customer eating habits. While many have not been successful, others have developed into large, profitable businesses.

Today in most cities and towns you can find several types of fast food businesses. They range from very small to very large, and from locally owned, independent businesses to regional and national chains and franchises.

While many people dream of opening their own restaurants, that opportunity is becoming increasingly difficult to achieve. In the fast food industry, menus are expanding, buildings are getting larger and more elaborate, specialized food-preparation equipment is used, large amounts of money are spent for promotion, and many people are needed to operate the business. It is not unusual for the owner of a fast food business to spend several hundred thousand dollars to open the business successfully.

However, it is also possible to start a fast food business on a smaller scale without a great deal of money. A small, specialized business may not have to compete directly with larger businesses and may be easier to manage. The same careful planning will be needed, however, with a small business as with a larger business.

This Continuing Project deals with the development of a small, specialized fast food business. You will make a series of decisions about the business and its potential for success in your community. In completing the activities, you will study the same information a person planning a new business would study. You will be making decisions that will allow you to determine if the business can be successful or not. After completing the entire project, you will have collected and analyzed the type of information needed to start and manage a small business. You will also have the satisfaction and confidence that you understand and can apply business principles and management concepts. You will also have a comprehensive set of materials that form a portfolio of your knowledge. You can personally be proud of that work and can show the portfolio to others as a way of demonstrating your achievement in *Business Principles and Management.*

## The Business

Hamburgers are an American tradition. At picnics, ball games, or for a quick lunch—hamburgers are a part of the eating habits of many people. Another tradition is the hamburger stand. The corner business or the street vendor that provides hamburgers with "all the fixings" has been a part of most neighborhoods for years. While many of the corner hamburger shops are gone, the tradition provides the basis for an inexpensive small business.

The Mobile Meals Company manufactures a product that can be used as a portable food stand. The food stand is actually a 3' x 4' x 3' aluminum box that is mounted on three wheels with a seat and handlebars so it can be pedaled like a bicycle. It is topped with a large, colorful umbrella. It contains a grill for cooking food that uses a safe propane heating element. In addition to the grill, the food stand has several compartments for food—two are heated, two are insulated. Smaller compartments hold containers for supplies and materials. A container for trash is located on the end of the stand away from the grill. The trash container has a hinged cover and can be separated from the cart to stand alone and for emptying.

The cost of the grill from Mobile Meals is $1,800. It can be purchased for cash or through a purchase contract in which you pay $50 a month for 48 months.

For the Continuing Project, you will start a small business by purchasing one of the portable food stands. You have decided to open a business that will sell hamburgers, warm pretzels and bagels, and cold lemonade from the stand. The hamburger stand will be pedaled to parks, athletic events, and other places where people gather. Mobile food stands such as the one you are planning have been successful when located at events and activities or in city shopping or business areas during lunch time.

To prepare for the Continuing Project, complete the following activities:

1. Develop a sketch of your hamburger stand. The sketch should show the food stand as it would appear to customers. You may want to decorate the umbrella and use other ways to make your hamburger stand attractive. Also diagram the work area of the food stand. Illustrate the grill; food and drink compartments; places for containers of catsup, pickles, relish, onions, mustard, etc.; and storage areas for supplies, utensils, and trash.

2. Develop a name for your business. A good business name should be short and easy to remember. It should relate to the type of business being operated, should be appealing to prospective customers, and different from other similar businesses. The name can be used on the umbrella or the side of the stand, and in later promotional activities that you will plan.

3. Assume that you will actually be opening and operating a business this year. Develop a time schedule that shows the seven days of the week. For each of the days on the schedule, identify the time you could usually devote to the planning and operation of the business. Total the hours to determine time you could devote to your own business each week.

4. Prepare a three-ring notebook for the project. The notebook will be used to maintain the records and information you develop while completing the activities for this project. You will often have to refer to previous decisions when completing new activities. The notebook will give you a permanent record of your decisions. Your teacher may have specific requirements for maintaining the project notebook and documenting your work.

5. If possible, complete the business planning activities using a computer and integrated business software program (word processing, spreadsheet, database, and graphics). Create files for each chapter or category of business decision making (organization, management, finance, marketing, etc.) and transfer information from one file to another as your business plans develop. Make sure to save back-up copies of all of your work.

6. Always study the related chapter first. It will provide background information, terminology, and sources of information for you to use as you complete the Continuing Project. You may want to return to the chapter or previous chapters to review information as you make specific decisions for your business.

7. Identify one or more business people who can serve as advisors for you during the time you are working on the project. Share the Continuing Project information with them so they are aware of the requirements. Meet and talk with them regularly to inform them about your coursework and your progress on the project. Ask for their help and advice in areas where you have difficulty locating information or where you are uncertain about decisions. Don't rely on the business person for the "correct" answer, but use his or her experience and knowledge as an important source of information to help you make decisions.

## Chapter 1 Activities

While fast food businesses are popular and successful today, you will want your business to be successful in the future. It is not practical to start a business that may not be needed in a few years. In this chapter you will be asked to study information to help you determine the future of your business.

### Data Collection

1. Review newspapers, magazines, and other publications to gather information about the size and growth of the fast food industry.
2. In your neighborhood, identify the types of fast food businesses that exist. Develop a list that includes the name of each business, the type of food, and the business location.
3. Find information that identifies the failure rate of new restaurants.

### Analysis

1. What factors have led to the growth of fast food businesses?
2. Is there any evidence that fast food businesses may not be as successful in the future?
3. What are the advantages and disadvantages of the portable hamburger stand as a new business in your community?

# Study Guide

**Part A**—*Directions:* Indicate your answer to each of the following questions by circling either yes or no in the Answers column.

| | | Answers | For Scoring |
|---|---|---|---|
| 1. | Does the United States have the world's largest economy? ........................... | yes no | 1. _____ |
| 2. | Do changes in population as well as changes in life styles directly affect business operations? ........................................................ | yes no | 2. _____ |
| 3. | In order for living standards to improve, must the country's population grow at a faster rate than its GDP? ........................................ | yes no | 3. _____ |
| 4. | Must a business consider both the size of the population and the nature of the population during its planning process? .................... | yes no | 4. _____ |
| 5. | Is the growth rate of a country controlled mostly by its birth rate? ............... | yes no | 5. _____ |
| 6. | Did the baby bust period create an increased supply of workers? ................... | yes no | 6. _____ |
| 7. | Will a business that specializes in selling goods for a particular age group be affected if the number of people in that age group greatly increases or decreases? | yes no | 7. _____ |
| 8. | Is the labor force defined as most people aged 16 or over who are available for work, whether employed or unemployed? ................................. | yes no | 8. _____ |
| 9. | In the last three decades, did the labor participation rate for women decrease? | yes no | 9. _____ |
| 10. | Has one of the problems of America's economy been its inability to create new jobs? ................................................................ | yes no | 10. _____ |
| 11. | Has the demand for skilled workers been falling? ......................................... | yes no | 11. _____ |
| 12. | Did a recent study reveal that the majority of adults were particularly deficient in math, computer, and communication skills? ................................ | yes no | 12. _____ |
| 13. | Has the United States Bureau of the Census found that about 25 percent of the population live in poverty? ........................................ | yes no | 13. _____ |
| 14. | Is it a generally accepted business principle that men should receive more pay than women for the same job? ........................................ | yes no | 14. _____ |
| 15. | Do businesses fear that comparable-worth programs will raise labor costs? ..... | yes no | 15. _____ |
| 16. | Does productivity tend to drop when employees regularly switch jobs? ......... | yes no | 16. _____ |
| 17. | Are resources such as natural gas, oil, and iron ore in unlimited supply? ........ | yes no | 17. _____ |
| 18. | When a business changes from natural gas to coal, does it meet environmental goals but violate conservation goals? .................................. | yes no | 18. _____ |
| 19. | Does ethical behavior relate to acceptable as well as unacceptable practices? .. | yes no | 19. _____ |
| 20. | Do codes of ethics often fail because they lack support from top-level managers? | yes no | 20. _____ |

**Part B—***Directions:* For each of the following statements, select the word, or group of words, that best completes the statement. In the Answers column, write the letter corresponding to the answer selected.

|  | Answers | For Scoring |
|---|---|---|

1. The point at which birth and death rates balance is called (a) balancing growth rate, (b) zero-population growth, (c) census rate growth, (d) leveling-off rate growth. ..........................................................     _____     1. _____

2. The number of workers employed in a recent year was approximately (a) 125 million, (b) 110 million, (c) 95 million, (d) 80 million. ......................     _____     2. _____

3. By the year 2000, the number of women in the labor force aged 20-54 is expected to increase by almost (a) 65%, (b) 75%, (c) 85%, (d) 95%. ................     _____     3. _____

4. With improved technology in recent years, the demand for skilled workers has (a) increased, (b) decreased a little, (c) remained about the same, (d) decreased a great deal. ..........................................................     _____     4. _____

5. Over the years, the labor-participation rate for men has (a) increased greatly, (b) increased slowly, (c) stayed about the same, (d) dropped greatly. ......................     _____     5. _____

6. Which of the following is NOT a factor in determining comparable worth? (a) Requiring special skills for a job. (b) Requiring certain educational backgrounds for a job. (c) Requiring certain physical ability for a job. (d) Requiring males or females for a job. ..........................................................     _____     6. _____

7. Which statement about the workforce is *incorrect*? (a) Women and racial minorities sometimes find it hard to be promoted above a certain level. (b) The pay for young workers is nearly equal for males and females but the gap widens with age. (c) Courts have favored comparable-worth plans. (d) An increasing number of women are entering traditionally male-dominated jobs. ............................     _____     7. _____

8. Which of the following is an *incorrect* statement regarding what employers are doing to attract and retain competent workers? (a) Improve the way work is done. (b) Assure healthier and safer working conditions. (c) Help workers deal with personal problems. (d) Train workers to like repetitive jobs. ..................     _____     8. _____

9. Which statement about the human factor in business is *false*? (a) Employees want more variety in their work. (b) Employees want more opportunity to participate in decisions that affect their working lives. (c) Employers are providing wellness programs. (d) Employees want less on-the-job responsibility. ...........     _____     9. _____

10. The U.S. Department of Labor predicts that (a) occupations demanding higher levels of education will grow slower than average, (b) the percentage of whites in the labor force will increase, (c) jobs for salespeople throughout the 1990s will increase, (d) jobs for company presidents will decrease. ...........................     _____     10. _____

**Part C—***Directions:* Below are listed several kinds of pollution. Indicate how each type of pollution should be classified by placing a check mark in the appropriate column.

|  | Water Pollution | Air Pollution | Land Pollution | For Scoring |
|---|---|---|---|---|
| 1. Exhaust being discharged by automobile engines. |  |  |  | 1. _____ |
| 2. Chemicals being dumped from a house into a sewer line. |  |  |  | 2. _____ |
| 3. Oil being spilled while being transported by an ocean liner. |  |  |  | 3. _____ |
| 4. A town's trash being dumped into an abandoned stone quarry. |  |  |  | 4. _____ |
| 5. Fish being killed by waste from a factory. |  |  |  | 5. _____ |

**Directions:** Study each controversial issue carefully. Follow the advice of your teacher before listing in the columns provided reasons why people might answer Yes or No. Your teacher may want you to work with a classmate, talk with others in your community to gather information, or use the library to gather facts.

2-1. Because most jobs require more skills than in the past, should the minimum amount of education be raised to 18 years or a high school diploma?

| Reasons for "Yes" | Reasons for "No" |
| --- | --- |
|  |  |

2-2. Should all firms be required to use the Valdez Principles rather than practicing the principles only on a voluntary basis? (The Valdez Principles appear in the textbook on page 41.)

| Reasons for "Yes" | Reasons for "No" |
| --- | --- |
|  |  |

# PROBLEMS

2-A. In a recent year, 92 million people worked in or near cities in the United States. Study the categories of jobs held by these people and answer the questions that follow. The figures are shown in millions of workers.

| | |
|---|---|
| Clerical | 15.8 |
| Professional | 13.6 |
| Managerial | 12.2 |
| Sales | 11.2 |
| Precision crafts | 9.9 |
| Service | 9.9 |
| Machinists | 5.5 |
| Technicians | 3.6 |
| Transportation | 3.4 |
| Laborers | 3.4 |
| Others | 3.4 |

1. What percent of the workforce applies to each of the top four job categories?

   a. Clerical _____

   b. Professional _____

   c. Managerial _____

   d. Sales _____

2. About what percent of the workforce do the top four job categories represent? _____

3. Which one job do you believe would be *most* likely to be held mainly by females? _____

4. Which one job do you believe would be *least* likely to be held mainly by females? _____

5. Which one job is *most* likely to be held by people with the fewest job skills? _____

2-B. The "baby busters" (busters) in a recent year who were aged 18-29 were compared with the entire population. The estimated breakdown by race is shown. Study the statistics and answer the questions that appear below the table. Note: Hispanics are also classified as white; therefore, totals will exceed 100%.

| | Baby Busters | Total Population |
|---|---|---|
| White | 81.2% | 83.5% |
| Black | 14.0 | 12.4 |
| American Indian | .9 | .8 |
| Asian | 3.9 | 3.3 |
| Hispanic | 12.3 | 9.5 |

1. What is the percentage difference of white busters in relation to the total white population? _____

2. What is the percentage difference of black busters in relation to the total black population? _____

3. Which race has the greatest percentage difference? _____

   What is the percentage difference? _____

4. What conclusion can be made about the difference between white busters and other busters?

   _____

**2-C.** In a recent year, the percent of the entire United States population living below the poverty level was 14.2 percent. Shown below are poverty levels for a sample of states. Study the figures and answer the questions.

| | |
|---|---|
| Michigan | 14.1% |
| Mississippi | 23.3% |
| Montana | 15.4% |
| Nevada | 11.4% |
| New Hampshire | 7.3% |
| New Mexico | 22.4% |
| Wisconsin | 9.9% |

1. Which states are in the Frost Belt? _____

_____

2. Which states are in the Sun Belt? _____

_____

3. Which one state can be most considered a Rust Belt state? _____

4. What is the average poverty level for the states shown?_____

5. How many times greater is the poverty level in Mississippi compared to New Hampshire's poverty level?

_____

6. For the average states shown, is the poverty level higher in the Frost Belt or the Sun Belt? _____

**2-D.** The yearly differences in pay between men and women with college degrees by age groups differ as shown below for a recent year. Study the figures and answer the questions.

| Age Group | Men | Women | Percent of Women's Pay to Men's Pay |
|---|---|---|---|
| 18-24 | $22,300 | $20,500 | _____ |
| 25-34 | 33,900 | 25,500 | _____ |
| 35-44 | 44,700 | 28,900 | _____ |
| 45-54 | 50,200 | 29,600 | _____ |
| 55-64 | 54,600 | 29,600 | _____ |

1. Calculate the percent of women's pay to men's pay and record your answers in the column shown above.
2. Provide three major reasons why the percent of women's pay to men's drops throughout one's working life.

a. _____

b. _____

c. _____

2-E. How aware are you of your environment? Answer the following questions as truthfully as possible about yourself and your family. Circle yes or no for each question. When you finish, check your environmental awareness score following the test.

1. Does your home or apartment have storm windows? ...................................... yes no 1. _____
2. Do your doors and windows have weather stripping or caulking? .................. yes no 2. _____
3. Is the thermostat lowered to 65 degrees or less when you go to bed? ............. yes no 3. _____
4. Do you turn off unnecessary lights when they are not being used? .................. yes no 4. _____
5. Is the thermostat in your home set no higher than 68 or 70 degrees when someone is there during the day? ......................................................... yes no 5. _____
6. Do you turn the water off while you brush your teeth? ................................. yes no 6. _____
7. Do you drink a glass of water immediately without running the water awhile first? ............................................................................................ yes no 7. _____
8. Are you aware that less water is used in a quick shower than in a bath? ......... yes no 8. _____
9. Are you aware that a self-defrosting refrigerator costs 25 percent more to operate? ............................................................................................ yes no 9. _____
10. Is there usually someone watching your television set while it is on? ............. yes no 10. _____
11. Do you place plastic containers, tins, newspapers and magazines in recycling containers instead of throwing them in the garbage? ................................... yes no 11. _____
12. Do you use a regular blanket rather than an electric blanket? ....................... yes no 12. _____
13. Is your family car (or cars) regularly maintained? ....................................... yes no 13. _____
14. Do you use sand rather than salt on icy roads, driveways, or sidewalks? ......... yes no 14. _____
15. When you take out fast food, do you regularly put the waste packaging such as wrappers and paper cups in waste containers? ............................................. yes no 15. _____
16. Do you compost leaves, grass clippings, and kitchen vegetable waste? ........... yes no 16. _____
17. When you buy your first car (or next car), will it be an economy car? ............. yes no 17. _____
18. Are you upset when you see litter, such as bottles, cans, and paper strewn about in your community? .......................................................................... yes no 18. _____
19. Do you discourage excessive purchase of food, clothes, and other items that you do not need? ................................................................................... yes no 19. _____
20. Do you, or would you, car pool to work? ................................................... yes no 20. _____

Count the number of *yes* answers and place your total score here. _____

If your total score is 16-20, you are *very alert* to your environment.
If your total score is 12-15, you are *fairly alert* to your environment.
If your total score is 8-11, you are *somewhat alert* to your environment.
If your total score is 0-7, you are *not alert* to your environment.

2-F. Businesses must be ethically responsible. For each situation, decide whether each business is "ethical" or "unethical." Circle your answer and give a reason for your decision.

1. Because the cost of hiring a firm to dispose of waste liquids from a paint manufacturing firm is so high, a company daily dumps a small amount into a nearby large river. The president knows that a very large business nearby also does this. "If they can do it, so can we," he says.

Decision: Ethical Unethical

Reason: _____

_____

2. A large company that sells apple juice and advertises it as "fresh" finds itself in financial difficulty. It decides to keep running the same ad but use imitation rather than real apple juice because people cannot tell the difference in taste. This action would allow the business to make enough profit to survive without having to fire some workers and cut other costs.

Decision: Ethical Unethical

Reason: _____

_____

3. Each December a small entrepreneur gives a sizable cash Christmas gift to key city officials with the hope that when special favors are needed, these officials will readily grant them. This is fairly common practice in this community.

Decision:  Ethical  Unethical

Reason: _____

_____


2-G. Read the following story and answer the questions that follow:

For years the Gumshoe Company has been doing rather well making house slippers for distribution by a large department store chain. Its 200 workers come from the small city of 75,000 in which the plant is located. Over 150 of the workers are women, most of whom work in the plant's cutting, sewing, and packaging departments. About 25 men work in the receiving and shipping department. There are about ten supervisors and managers, all of whom are males. The rest of the employees are office, maintenance, and design people. Last week the plant manager, Barry Danziger, received the following typewritten message:

```
Sir: For too long this company has been run by men who keep women in
their place. Sexist comments are heard frequently and, worst of all, not
a single woman holds a management position. None of us is ever considered
for a supervisory position when an opening occurs. Someone from the
shipping and receiving department always gets it. We expect the next
supervisory position that opens to be filled by a woman, or you will
immediately see that we mean business.
                                             Women's Rights Committee
```

Mr. Danziger asked the present supervisors what they knew about the matter. None had heard anything. Some of the more outspoken women workers were also contacted. All remained silent. Barry Danziger was puzzled. All management openings are announced through a newsletter and posted on plant bulletin boards. When the last opening occurred, not a single woman had applied.

1. What action could the women take to show management that they "mean business"? _____

_____


2. Give two possible reasons why no woman applied for the last supervisory position. _____

_____


3. If no women from the plant apply for the next position, what should the plant manager do? _____

_____

_____

_____

_____

_____

_____

_____

2-H. Assume you are an employee in a company where the business situations described below have occurred. Check your decision in the ethical or unethical column that appears on the right and give a reason for your decision.

Ethical    Unethical

1. A co-worker was absent from work yesterday to visit a friend but plans to report it as an illness. .................................................................... _____    _____

   Reason: _____

   _____

2. Your boss plans to overstate your department's output so that she will win the Manager of the Month award. ....................................................... _____    _____

   Reason: _____

   _____

3. You learn that the business has an old warehouse that is no longer needed for storage. Management has decided to make offices there for fifty clerks. The building's walls have asbestos that could harm workers over time. ................................... _____    _____

   Reason: _____

   _____

4. A product your firm makes is dangerous to users but the firm plans to take no action to make the item safe. ................................................... _____    _____

   Reason: _____

   _____

5. Another employee has been using illegal drugs on the job and the supervisor does not know about it. ......................................................... _____    _____

   Reason: _____

   _____

6. A salesperson has the use of a company car but you have seen the car used on weekends for personal use. ....................................................... _____    _____

   Reason: _____

   _____

7. A highly qualified African American worker applied for an opening as a supervisor but was rejected in favor of a less-qualified white candidate. ............................ _____    _____

   Reason: _____

   _____

8. A less-qualified black male was promoted to a managerial position over a more highly qualified white female. ......................................................... _____    _____

   Reason: _____

   _____

# CONTINUING PROJECT
## Chapter 2 Activities

The way people in a community view a business can often determine whether it will be successful or not. Changes in population, income, attitudes, and values must be considered by a business owner. In this chapter, you will study the social environment in which your business will operate and the importance of ethical operations to business success.

### Data Collection

1. Collect newspaper and magazine articles that describe social and environmental changes that could affect your business.
2. Interview five people of various ages and backgrounds. Ask them to describe their positive and negative feelings about fast food businesses.
3. Discuss the importance of ethics in business with several business owners. Ask them to identify the areas of business operations where ethics is most important.
4. Contact government agencies in your community to identify local recycling regulations that will affect your type of business as well as laws that must be observed.

### Analysis

1. Develop a set of operating rules and procedures for your business that will demonstrate to the citizens of the community that you are concerned about their feelings, will operate ethically, and have a sense of social responsibility. Examples: use of resources, pollution, ethics, quality.
2. Identify two social trends that you believe will have a positive impact on your business and two that could have a negative effect. For each trend, indicate what you can do within the operation of your business to take advantage of the positive factors and to overcome the negative factors.
3. Develop a short code of ethics including statements on rules of conduct with customers, other businesses, and employees of the business.
4. Identify several ethical dilemmas you might face in buying or selling your fast food products and disposing of waste materials. For each dilemma, describe how you will resolve it in an ethical way.

# Study Guide

**Part A**—*Directions:* Indicate your answer to each of the following questions by circling either yes or no in the Answers column.

|  | | Answers | For Scoring |
|---|---|---|---|

1. Is the body of knowledge that relates to producing and using goods and services to satisfy human wants known as economics? ............................................... yes   no   1. _____
2. Does our economic system concern itself with all the wants of the people? ..... yes   no   2. _____
3. Is a glass of water an economic want? ............................................... yes   no   3. _____
4. Does a retail grocer provide both time utility and place utility? ................... yes   no   4. _____
5. Is a robot on a car assembly line an example of a consumer good? ................. yes   no   5. _____
6. Are capital goods needed to produce consumer goods and services? .............. yes   no   6. _____
7. Can a country produce as many capital goods as it wishes to produce at any one time? ................................................................................................ yes   no   7. _____
8. If the production of consumer goods increases, must the production of capital goods and services also increase? ....................................................... yes   no   8. _____
9. Are countries that normally adopt a market economy often dictatorships? ..... yes   no   9. _____
10. Does privatization occur when a country provides a good or service that was formerly provided by a business? ...................................................... yes   no   10. _____
11. As the demand for a product decreases, does the price of the product usually increase? ......................................................................................... yes   no   11. _____
12. Can a change in the demand or the supply of a product cause a change in the price of a product? ........................................................................... yes   no   12. _____
13. Do consumers help decide what will be produced as well as how much will be produced? ........................................................................................ yes   no   13. _____
14. Is competition among businesses limited mainly to price competition? ......... yes   no   14. _____
15. Is it necessary to expand only the production of goods and services for economic growth to occur? ............................................................................. yes   no   15. _____
16. Will a decrease in production and an increase in unemployment occur during recessions? ........................................................................................ yes   no   16. _____
17. Is a recession a slowdown or a decline in the GNP that continues for three months or more? .................................................................................. yes   no   17. _____
18. Is inflation accompanied by a decline in the purchasing power of money? ...... yes   no   18. _____
19. During inflation, does the dollar buy more than it did before inflation? ........ yes   no   19. _____
20. Does the lowering and raising of taxes by the federal government aid in controlling recession and inflation? ............................................................ yes   no   20. _____

**Part B**—*Directions:* For each of the following statements, select the word, or group of words, that best completes the statement. In the Answers column, write the letter corresponding to the answer selected.

|  | Answers | For Scoring |
|---|---|---|

1. Which of the following is NOT considered an economic want? (a) want for a television set, (b) want for medical attention, (c) want for friendship, (d) want for new clothing. .................................................................... _____ 1. _____

2. A shoe manufacturer creates (a) form utility, (b) time utility, (c) place utility, (d) economic utility. ................................................................... _____ 2. _____

3. When the production of consumer goods decreases, the production of (a) capital goods increases, (b) capital goods and services increases, (c) capital goods decreases, (d) capital goods and services decreases. .............................. _____ 3. _____

4. The basic factors of production are (a) natural resources and labor; (b) natural resources, labor, and capital goods; (c) natural resources, labor, capital goods, and management; (d) capital goods and labor. ............................... _____ 4. _____

5. Machines used to make automobiles are classified as (a) consumer goods, (b) capital goods, (c) consumer services, (d) domestic goods. .......................... _____ 5. _____

6. What type of economy is most typically found in China? (a) capital, (b) command, (c) market, (d) mixed. .......................................................... _____ 6. _____

7. In which type of economy do consumers and producers act independently to determine what, how, and for whom goods and services are produced? (a) communistic, (b) command, (c) market, (d) mixed. ..................................... _____ 7. _____

8. The term that best describes our present economic/political system is (a) socialism, (b) communism, (c) capitalism, (d) privatization. ................................ _____ 8. _____

9. Approximately what percent of total receipts represents the average net profit of all business firms? (a) 5%, (b) 10%, (c) 15%, (d) 25%. ............................ _____ 9. _____

10. Demand for a product is the (a) same as want, (b) price at which the product will sell most readily, (c) number of products that will be bought at a given time at a given price, (d) number of future customers. .................................. _____ 10. _____

11. Prices are determined by the forces of (a) supply only, (b) demand only, (c) both supply and demand, (d) business cycles. ............................................. _____ 11. _____

12. Nonprice competition occurs when a firm (a) takes business away from its competitors by lowering prices, (b) conducts an extensive advertising campaign to convince the public that its product is better than all other brands, (c) does not have to compete with other sellers for consumer dollars, (d) occurs only when service is provided. ................................................................... _____ 12. _____

13. Economic growth occurs when a country produces goods and services at (a) the same rate the population is increasing, (b) a faster rate than the population is increasing, (c) a slower rate than the population is increasing, (d) the same rate unemployment is increasing. ............................................................ _____ 13. _____

14. The Consumer Price index (CPI) is best defined as (a) the total market value of all goods produced and services purchased in a year, (b) the total of all the products that are purchased at a given time, (c) a measure of the average change in prices of consumer goods and services, (d) the same as the Economic Index of Leading Indicators. ............................................................... _____ 14. _____

15. Which of the following is NOT likely to occur during a recession? (a) decreased production, (b) increased unemployment, (c) increased demand for goods and services, (d) rapid rise in the CPI. ................................................... _____ 15. _____

**Directions:** Study each controversial issue carefully. Follow the advice of your teacher before listing in the columns provided reasons why people might answer Yes or No. Your teacher may want you to work with a classmate, talk with others in your community to gather information, or use the library to gather facts.

3-1. Should the federal government privatize the U.S. Postal Service?

| Reasons for "Yes" | Reasons for "No" |
| --- | --- |
| | |

3-2. In order to encourage savings and, in turn, capital formation, should the interest earned by individuals on savings and other investments NOT be taxed by the federal government?

| Reasons for "Yes" | Reasons for "No" |
| --- | --- |
| | |

# PROBLEMS

**3-A.** In economics, *utility* is the ability of a good or service to satisfy a want. For each of the four common types of utility shown in the columns below, check the one type of utility that best fits the situation described.

|  | *Types of Utility* | | | |
|---|---|---|---|---|
|  | Form | Place | Time | Possession |
| 1. You go to a nearby store to buy a canvas walking shoe, but the store carries leather only. ............................................... | _____ | _____ | _____ | _____ |
| 2. You have just completed signing the rental form for the use of a portable computer to take on a business trip. ............... | _____ | _____ | _____ | _____ |
| 3. You dash into a bookstore on your lunch hour and ask for this week's best selling novel by name, which the clerk has in stock. ............................................................................ | _____ | _____ | _____ | _____ |
| 4. You were planning to walk home after a movie, but it is raining so you look for a taxi. One pulls up as you leave the theater. ............................................................................ | _____ | _____ | _____ | _____ |

**3-B.** For each item listed below, determine whether it is a capital good or a consumer good. Check the appropriate column.

|  | Capital Good | Consumer Good |
|---|---|---|
| 1. Bulldozer for building contractors ....... | _____ | _____ |
| 2. Garden hose ..................................... | _____ | _____ |
| 3. Home ............................................... | _____ | _____ |
| 4. Factory ............................................. | _____ | _____ |
| 5. Machines for making bicycles .............. | _____ | _____ |

**3-C.** For each situation described below, check the column indicating whether it represents a demand or a want.

|  | Demand | Want |
|---|---|---|
| 1. A youngster would like a particular toy but does not have quite enough money to buy it. ................................................................................... | _____ | _____ |
| 2. A small business owner would like to install a new, plush rug in the customer waiting room but has not fully decided whether to spend that much money on it. | _____ | _____ |
| 3. An apartment dweller is waiting for the next big sale so that a vacuum cleaner that is nearly worn out can be replaced. ................................................. | _____ | _____ |
| 4. A college graduate plans to purchase on credit several new business suits, which will be needed when reporting to a new job in several weeks. ............................ | _____ | _____ |

**3-D.** On the line provided, write the name of the economic system that best represents each statement.

1. Resources are allocated by government only. _____

2. Marketing decisions are made by market conditions. _____

3. China is a good example of this economic system. _____

4. Businesses and individuals own natural resources and capital goods. _____

5. Government controls business decisions extensively for the allocation of some resources, but little over distribution. _____

**3-E.** For each economic-political system listed, check the column that best fits its characteristics.

| | Capitalism | Socialism | Communism |
|---|---|---|---|
| 1. Freedom to own land and other property. | ____ | ____ | ____ |
| 2. Usually a shortage of consumer goods. | ____ | ____ | ____ |
| 3. Some industries owned by government but consumers decide what other goods are produced. | ____ | ____ | ____ |
| 4. Nearly any individual may start a business. | ____ | ____ | ____ |
| 5. Government decides how and what goods are to be produced | ____ | ____ | ____ |

**3-F.** Below are a few average prices shown in 1993 dollars for goods and services for three different time periods. Study the figures and answer the questions.

|  | In 1993 dollars | | |
|---|---|---|---|
| | 1953 | 1973 | 1993 |
| Gallon of gas | 1.55 | 1.26 | 1.12 |
| Movie ticket (New York City) | 2.75 | 5.74 | 5.05 |
| Television (color) | 1,432* | 1,466 | 220 |
| Hospital cost for one day | 108 | 332 | 752 |
| Eggs (one dozen) | 3.77 | 2.54 | .89 |
| Postage (first-class letter) | .16 | .26 | .29 |

*Only available in black and white.*

1. Which items declined in price? _____

2. What economic factors might have most influenced the price of the items that declined in price? _____

3. Provide a possible reason why the price of movie tickets went up in 1973 but dropped in 1993. _____

4. If car manufacturers are able to produce engines that use half as much gas, what might happen to the price of gas twenty years from now? _____

5. By what percent did the cost of eggs decrease from 1953 to 1993? _____

6. By what percent did the cost of postage on a first-class letter increase from 1953 to 1993? _____

3-G. Study the Consumer Price Index figures below for two different years. Then answer the questions below.

|  | Year #5* | Year #15* |
|---|---|---|
| Food and beverages | 188.0 | 302.0 |
| Housing | 164.5 | 349.9 |
| Apparel and upkeep | 142.3 | 206.0 |
| Transportation | 150.6 | 319.9 |
| Medical care | 168.6 | 403.1 |
| Entertainment | 152.2 | 265.0 |
| Other goods and services | 153.9 | 326.6 |

*In Year #1 the CPI was 100.

1. Which item had the greatest increase in the CPI during the ten-year period? _____

2. Which item had the least increase in the CPI during the decade? _____

3. As the CPI increases, does the purchasing power of the dollar increase, decrease, or stay about the same?

_____

4. What types of people are hurt most by rapid increases in the CPI? _____

5. Are increases in the CPI a measure of the rate of inflation, recession, or depression? _____

6. When the GNP is growing at a desirable rate, is the CPI likely to be increasing also? _____

3-H. If the national economy grows too fast, the result may be inflation. But if it grows too slowly, a recession or a depression is likely to occur. The federal government may take different actions that can help control the economy by controlling the rate of growth. Place a check in one of the columns on the right to show the expected effect of each governmental action on the economy.

|  | Speeds Economic Growth | Slows Economic Growth | No Effect on Economic Growth |
|---|---|---|---|
| 1. Raising federal income taxes | _____ | _____ | _____ |
| 2. Lowering federal income taxes | _____ | _____ | _____ |
| 3. Increasing government spending for transportation | _____ | _____ | _____ |
| 4. Reducing government spending for defense | _____ | _____ | _____ |
| 5. Launching a new satellite to the planet Venus | _____ | _____ | _____ |
| 6. Passing a new law to lower the voting age | _____ | _____ | _____ |

3-I. Most nations experience business cycles. Check the appropriate business cycle phase shown in the columns on the right with the situation described on the left.

|  | Expansion | Peak | Contraction | Trough |
|---|---|---|---|---|
| 1. A period when unemployment is at its worst. | _____ | _____ | _____ | _____ |
| 2. A period of high employment and rising wages and prices. | _____ | _____ | _____ | _____ |
| 3. A period called depression. | _____ | _____ | _____ | _____ |
| 4. A period just before the unemployment rate starts to climb. | _____ | _____ | _____ | _____ |
| 5. A period of runaway inflation. | _____ | _____ | _____ | _____ |
| 6. A period when prices stop rising and graduates begin to find it more difficult to land jobs. | _____ | _____ | _____ | _____ |

3-J. Obtain three brands of ballpoint pens, or some other low-priced product that most people buy from time to time. Select brands that differ in price, color, size, or shape. Ask ten people which item they would buy if they needed a pen and if these were the only choices. Once each person has selected the brand, ask for the main reason for the selection. Record the information below and answer the questions that follow.

|  | Brand A | Brand B | Brand C |
|---|---|---|---|
| Brand or Product Preference: | ____ | ____ | ____ |

Main Reason for Selecting Brand A, Brand B, or Brand C

|  | Brand A | Brand B | Brand C |
|---|---|---|---|
| Price | ____ | ____ | ____ |
| Color | ____ | ____ | ____ |
| Size | ____ | ____ | ____ |
| Shape | ____ | ____ | ____ |
| Quality | ____ | ____ | ____ |
| Reputation of Company | ____ | ____ | ____ |
| Other (write in) _____ | ____ | ____ | ____ |

1. Which brand was the most popular? _____

2. Which brand was the least popular? _____

3. What was the main reason for selecting the most popular brand? _____

_____

4. Did price or nonprice competition most often influence potential buyers? _____

# CONTINUING PROJECT
## Chapter 3 Activities

A new business owner must be aware of the type of competition the business will face and the strengths and weaknesses of that competition. Also, customer demand for the business' products needs to be determined. Those factors will be studied in this chapter.

### Data Collection

1. Use the chart developed in the Chapter 1 Continuing Project that lists the fast food businesses in the area where you live. For each business, identify strengths in one column and weaknesses in another column (be as objective as possible). Rate each business on the basis of variety of products, location, prices, service, and image.
2. Identify five products that appear on the menus of most fast food businesses. Visit the businesses in your area and determine the highest and lowest prices being charged for each item.
3. Interview ten people to determine how price affects their purchase decisions. Ask the following questions and summarize the responses.
   a. How much would you usually expect to pay for a hamburger? A bagel? A hot pretzel? A glass of lemonade?
   b. How important is the price when you decide to buy any of those products?
   c. What factors would cause you to pay a higher-than-normal price for any of the products?

### Analysis

1. A business must be able to satisfy consumer needs in order to be successful. Describe how your new business will provide the four basic utilities discussed in the textbook: form, place, time, and possession.
2. Identify several specific ways you can reduce the level of competition or increase the customer demand for your products.
3. How important do you think prices of your products will be to the success of your business? What is the evidence to support your decision? How might changes in the economy affect the amount you can charge for your products?
4. Make initial pricing decisions for each of your products. (You may decide to change them later.) Provide a rationale for the prices you set, including the factors you used to set each price.

| Chapter 4 | | Scoring Record | | | | |
|---|---|---|---|---|---|---|
| | Name _____ | | Part A | Part B | Part C | Total |
| International Environment of Business | | Perfect score | 20 | 10 | 5 | 35 |
| | Date _____ | My score | | | | |

# Study Guide

**Part A**—*Directions:* Indicate your answer to each of the following questions by circling either yes or no in the Answers column.

| | | Answers | | For Scoring |
|---|---|---|---|---|
| 1. | Because of the growth of international trade, do most countries operate under the same rules and regulations? .................................................. | yes | no | 1. _____ |
| 2. | Have trade patterns on an international level shifted from services to goods?.. | yes | no | 2. _____ |
| 3. | Are approximately four percent of American workers employed by foreign countries that operate in the United States? ......................................... | yes | no | 3. _____ |
| 4. | Does a parent firm refer to a business that owns production and service facilities outside the country in which it is based? ....................................... | yes | no | 4. _____ |
| 5. | Are most of the world's smallest corporations multinationals? ...................... | yes | no | 5. _____ |
| 6. | Do sales level off during the maturity stage of a product? ........................... | yes | no | 6. _____ |
| 7. | Do American companies move to foreign countries when sales at home begin to grow? .................................................................................. | yes | no | 7. _____ |
| 8. | Does a balance of trade deficit exist when more money leaves a country than comes in? ............................................................................... | yes | no | 8. _____ |
| 9. | Are goods and services purchased from other countries called imports? .......... | yes | no | 9. _____ |
| 10. | By 1991, was the United States able to turn its prior trade deficits into trade surpluses? ............................................................................... | yes | no | 10. _____ |
| 11. | Might countries with prolonged trade deficits have to restrict the activities of foreign businesses in their countries? ......................................... | yes | no | 11. _____ |
| 12. | When the demand for foreign currency decreases, does the value of the dollar increase? ............................................................................... | yes | no | 12. _____ |
| 13. | Are tariffs imposed in order for a country to earn revenue? ......................... | yes | no | 13. _____ |
| 14. | Do tariffs raise the price of foreign products? ........................................ | yes | no | 14. _____ |
| 15. | Does dumping lower the price of goods sold in a foreign market? ................ | yes | no | 15. _____ |
| 16. | Do quotas limit the number of goods permitted to enter a country? ............. | yes | no | 16. _____ |
| 17. | Should non-tariff barriers increase the number of imports that enter a country? | yes | no | 17. _____ |
| 18. | Are governments allowed to restrict investments made by foreigners? .......... | yes | no | 18. _____ |
| 19. | Does a trading block discourage free trade among its members? .................... | yes | no | 19. _____ |
| 20. | Do Americans export goods from France when they buy French perfume? ..... | yes | no | 20. _____ |

**Part B**—*Directions:* For each of the following statements, select the word, or group of words, that best completes the statement. In the Answers column, write the letter corresponding to the answer selected.

|  | Answers | For Scoring |
|---|---|---|

1. Which nation is NOT included as part of the Pacific Rim? (a) China, (b) Hong Kong, (c) Taiwan, (d) South America. ........................................ _____ 1. _____

2. In a recent year, foreigners owned 14 percent of the assets and employed one in seven workers in (a) Japan, (b) Great Britain, (c) Mexico, (d) France. ............ _____ 2. _____

3. In order to gain a trade advantage, a country specializes in a product it can provide more efficiently than other countries. What theory is that country practicing? (a) balance of trade, (b) comparative advantage theory, (c) product life cycle theory, (d) balance of surplus theory. ...................................... _____ 3. _____

4. The first two stages that a product goes through are the (a) introductory and growth stages, (b) introductory and decline stages, (c) growth and maturity stages, (d) growth and decline stages. ...................................... _____ 4. _____

5. Over the past 20 years, what has happened to U.S. exports and imports? (a) Exports exceeded imports. (b) Imports exceeded exports. (c) Imports equaled exports. (d) Exports jumped dramatically. ...................................... _____ 5. _____

6. If the Canadians keep increasing the number of American cars purchased, (a) American products will become more expensive for Canadians, (b) Canadian products will become more expensive for Americans, (c) American products will become less expensive for Canadians, (d) Canadian products will become less expensive for Americans. ...................................... _____ 6. _____

7. How do tariffs affect the prices of foreign goods? (a) Prices increase. (b) Prices decrease. (c) Prices remain the same. (d) Prices fluctuate at a quick pace. ....... _____ 7. _____

8. If the United States sets a tariff of 15 percent on $150 cameras that are made in Germany, the cost of the camera in the U.S. will rise to (a) $155.50, (b) $165, (c) $172.50, (d) $175. ...................................... _____ 8. _____

9. Non-tariff barriers (a) increase the number of imports that enter a country, (b) increase the value of one currency to another, (c) protect domestic producers, (d) protect foreign producers. ...................................... _____ 9. _____

10. Which of the following treaties is NOT meant to govern international trade? (a) GATT, (b) GDP, (c) IMF, (d) World Bank. ...................................... _____ 10. _____

**Part C**—*Directions:* In the Answers column, write the letter of the word or expression in Column I that most closely matches each statement in Column II.

| Column I | Column II | Answers | For Scoring |
|---|---|---|---|
| A. Balance of trade | 1. An example of a trade bloc. ...................................... | _____ | 1. _____ |
| B. Dumping | 2. Restrictions on quantities permitted to enter a country. ...................................... | _____ | 2. _____ |
| C. EU | 3. Selling goods below cost in a foreign market. .......... | _____ | 3. _____ |
| D. Exports | 4. Goods and services purchased from other countries. . | _____ | 4. _____ |
| E. Free trade | 5. Difference between money coming into and going out of a country. ...................................... | _____ | 5. _____ |
| F. Imports |  |  |  |
| G. Quotas |  |  |  |

Name _____

**Directions:** Study each controversial issue carefully. Follow the advice of your teacher before listing in the columns provided reasons why people might answer Yes or No. Your teacher may want you to work with a classmate, talk with others in your community to gather information, or use the library to gather facts.

4-1. Should South America form a trading bloc that might be called SAFTA (South American Free Trade Association)?

| Reasons for "Yes" | Reasons for "No" |
| --- | --- |
|  |  |

4-2. Because of the growing importance of international trade and relations, should all students be required to study a foreign language and take a course dealing with world cultures?

| Reasons for "Yes" | Reasons for "No" |
| --- | --- |
|  |  |

# PROBLEMS

**4-A.** Listed below are the names of ten of the world's largest firms. Use the library and other sources to name the home country and the main industry or product for each.

| Company | Country | Industry |
|---|---|---|
| Aerospatiale | _____ | _____ |
| Barlow Rand | _____ | _____ |
| Citizen Watch | _____ | _____ |
| E. I. DuPont de Nemours | _____ | _____ |
| Electrolux | _____ | _____ |
| Hyundai Motor | _____ | _____ |
| Northern Telecom | _____ | _____ |
| Petrofina | _____ | _____ |
| Siemans | _____ | _____ |
| Smithkline Beecham | _____ | _____ |

**4-B.** Listed below is the value of exports shown in millions of dollars for three fictitious countries for selected products. Study the figures and answer the questions that follow.

|  | Galafo | Minion | Ungwa |
|---|---|---|---|
| Lumber | $1,350 | $ 700 | $ 0 |
| Coffee | 50 | 7,000 | 850 |
| Rice | 920 | 250 | 6,900 |
| Fish | 530 | 610 | 490 |

1. Which country is likely to have the competitive advantage for each of the following products?

   a. Lumber _____

   b. Coffee _____

   c. Rice _____

2. How could Galafo best trade with Minion? _____

3. How could Minion best trade with Ungwa? _____

4. If Ungwa had an embargo on Galafo's lumber, what might Ungwa do to obtain lumber? _____

_____

_____

_____

4-C. The following chart shows the cost for selected products available to customers in four major world cities in a recent year. Study the chart and answer the questions below.

|  | New York | London | Tokyo | Mexico City |
|---|---|---|---|---|
| Compact disc | $12.99 | $14.99 | $22.09 | $13.91 |
| Movie | 7.50 | 10.50 | 17.29 | 4.55 |
| Sony Walkman (mid-range) | 59.95 | 74.98 | 211.34 | 110.00 |
| Cup of coffee | 1.25 | 1.50 | 2.80 | .91 |
| Designer jeans | 39.99 | 74.92 | 79.73 | 54.54 |
| Nike Air Jordans | 125.00 | 134.99 | 172.91 | 154.24 |

1. If you lived in Japan, which city would you most like to visit to get the best buys for your money?

   _____

2. If you did not live in any of the countries represented by these cities, in which city would you least like to visit if you decided to go on a shopping spree to buy some of the items listed above? _____

3. What percentage more would an American pay for a movie in London than in the U.S.? _____

4. What percentage less would an American pay for a movie in Mexico City? _____

5. What purchasing advice would you give to an American who wants to travel to London?

   _____

   _____

   _____

4-D. Indicate whether each situation described below is an embargo, tariff, quota, ban, or non-tariff barrier.

|  | Embargo | Tariff | Quota | Ban | Non-Tariff Barrier |
|---|---|---|---|---|---|
| 1. The United States limits the number of Japanese cars that may be imported each year... | ___ | ___ | ___ | ___ | ___ |
| 2. The Japanese do not permit the importing of certain American products. ..................... | ___ | ___ | ___ | ___ | ___ |
| 3. American producers are not allowed to sell materials to North Koreans that are used to make nuclear bombs. ..................... | ___ | ___ | ___ | ___ | ___ |
| 4. France places a tax on alcoholic beverages imported from the United States. .................... | ___ | ___ | ___ | ___ | ___ |
| 5. Some countries do not buy VCRs from many producers because they are made mostly in black, which is the color of death. .................... | ___ | ___ | ___ | ___ | ___ |
| 6. Action the United States might take if a firm in a foreign country attempted to dump its products here. ..................... | ___ | ___ | ___ | ___ | ___ |

**4-E.** In a recent year, the U.S. Department of Commerce reported the following figures on imports and exports of selected products in millions of dollars. Study the figures and answer the questions that follow.

|  | Exports | Imports |
|---|---|---|
| Coffee | $ 9.8 | $1,735.6 |
| Rice | 752.2 | 80.3 |
| Wheat | 3,348.1 | 66.1 |
| Clothing | 3,211.6 | 26,205.8 |
| Motorcycles/bicycles | 1,302.6 | 1,635.9 |
| Scientific instruments | 13,487.6 | 6,757.4 |
| Total | _____ | _____ |

1. Calculate the total exports and imports and record each total in the space provided.

2. By how much did the imports exceed the exports? _____

3. Which goods are imported in greater quantity than exported? _____

4. Which goods are exported in greater quantity than imported? _____

5. Based on these products only, does a balance of trade surplus or deficit exist? _____

6. Which one item most contributed to the difference between the total imports and exports? _____

**4-F.** Here are exchange rates for one American dollar in a recent year for four countries.

|  | Year #1 | Year #2 |
|---|---|---|
| Canadian dollar | $1.28 | $1.37 |
| French franc | 5.69 | 5.56 |
| Japanese yen | 1.06 | 1.12 |
| Mexican peso | 3.35 | 3.13 |

1. Assume you bought the following products while vacationing over the last two years. Determine how much you paid in American dollars in the currency of the country you visited.

a. Camera for 150 Canadian dollars (Year #1) _____

b. Perfume for 110 French francs (Year #2) _____

c. Jewelry for 50 Mexican pesos (Year #1) _____

2. Assume you bought binoculars in Japan in Year #1 for 87 yen and in Year #2 you returned to Japan for a second visit and you saw the item at the same store for 115 yen.

a. In Year #1, what was it worth in American dollars? _____

b. What was the dollar price in Year #2? _____

**4-G.** Many countries belong to trading blocs. Place a check mark in the column at the right to indicate whether the country is a member of the European Union (EU), North American Free Trade Association (NAFTA), or neither.

|  | EU | NAFTA | Neither |
|---|---|---|---|
| 1. Greece | ____ | ____ | ____ |
| 2. Britain | ____ | ____ | ____ |
| 3. Mexico | ____ | ____ | ____ |
| 4. Japan | ____ | ____ | ____ |
| 5. Canada | ____ | ____ | ____ |
| 6. Brazil | ____ | ____ | ____ |
| 7. Italy | ____ | ____ | ____ |

**4-H.** Assume that you have been working in an American company for several years and you now have the opportunity to work in one of its branch offices located in another country. Answer the following questions before you leave for your new job abroad.

1. Provide the name of the country to which you wish to be assigned. _____

2. Why did you select this country? _____

   _____

3. What is the currency and how many units of that currency are equal to one American dollar? _____

   _____

4. Assume that your salary in the United States is $25,000 a year. What is it worth in the currency of your

   new country? _____

5. What are two main products that this country exports? _____

6. What are two main imports of this country? _____

7. What is the language of your new country? _____

8. Write the following sentence in the language of the country: "My name is ... and I live in the United States

   of America."

   _____

9. What are the average temperatures for the following months:

   June _____    October _____

   January _____    March _____

10. Identify several different customs practiced in this country regarding such items as being on time for

    appointments, working hours, table etiquette, popular food dishes, eye contact, dress, holidays, and reli-

    gion.

    _____

    _____

    _____

# CONTINUING PROJECT
## Chapter 4 Activities

While new, small businesses seldom consider the impact of international business on their operations, almost all businesses today operate in an international business environment. Many suppliers of products and services purchased by small businesses are international businesses or are owned by businesses located in other countries. A foreign market becomes less foreign as a person learns more about it. A business owner needs to study those markets in order to understand potential foreign business opportunities. A small business that carefully researches a foreign market can be just as successful in international markets as a large business.

### Data Collection

1. Identify several businesses in the fast food industry that are heavily involved in international trade or are multinational businesses. Identify the products they manufacture or market and the primary countries in which they operate.

2. Collect information on recent trade agreements and legislation that deal with international business. Summarize what experts are predicting the affect of the agreements and laws will have on U.S. businesses.

3. If you have access to people who have lived in other countries, discuss the types of fast food businesses they are familiar with in the country in which they lived. Identify similarities and differences from the typical fast food operations in the United States.

### Analysis

1. Identify three ways that international trade by U.S. businesses can have a positive affect on small businesses and three ways it can have a negative affect on those businesses.

2. Identify several food products popular in other countries and cultures you would consider as additions to your product line. They must fit the requirements of being prepared and sold from the mobile cart.

3. Assume that you have operated your business for 15 years, and it has been very successful in the United States. You now have franchises in 30 states. You want to test the international market to see if the business will work in other countries. Identify at least two countries that you would consider to introduce your business. Outline the steps you would follow to determine if international operations would be successful in those countries.

Name *Evar Jones*

## Partnership Agreement

THIS CONTRACT, Made and entered into on the (1.) *First* day of (2.) 19 *June* by and between (3.) *Jennifer L. York, party of the first part, Robert R. Burton, of Buffalo*

WITNESSES: That the said parties have this day formed a copartnership for the purpose of engaging in and conducting (4.) *Grocery - fruit - meat market and bakery*

business under the following stipulations, which are made a part of the contract:

FIRST: The said copartnership is to continue for a term of (5.) *Ten years* from date hereof.

SECOND: The business shall be conducted under the firm name of (6.) *Y, B, and C Fine Foods* at (7.) *4467 Goodson St, Buffalo, New York*

THIRD: The investments are as follows: (8.) *Henry: $40,000, Shaw: $30,000*

FOURTH: All profits or losses arising from said business are to be divided as follows: (9.) *Shared proportionately to the investment of the partners*

FIFTH: Each partner is to devote his or her entire time and attention to the business and to engage in no other business enterprise without the written consent of the other.

SIXTH: Each partner is to have a salary of (10.) $ *2,000* a month, the same to be withdrawn at such time or times as he or she may elect. Neither partner is to withdraw from the business an amount in excess of his or her salary without the written consent of the other.

SEVENTH: The duties of each partner are defined as follows. (11.) *Henry is to have general supervision of television repairs, Shaw is to be in charge of all other electronic repairs.*

EIGHTH: Neither partner is to become surety or bondsperson for anyone without the written consent of the other.

NINTH: (12.) _____

TENTH: (13.) _____

IN WITNESS WHEREOF, The parties aforesaid have hereunto set their hands and affixed their seals on the day and year above written.

(14.) _____

(15.) _____

5-H. Answer the following questions about the partnership of Thomas Henry and Marie Shaw in Problem 5-G:

1. After the salaries to the partners have been paid, the profits for a particular year amounted to $37,800.

   Henry's share will be  $_____   Shaw's share will be  $_____

2. Since Henry has the larger investment in the partnership, does he have more authority than Shaw in

   deciding how to operate the business? _____

3. Without Shaw's knowledge, Henry placed an order for ten television sets of a new make. Will the partner-

   ship be bound by this contract? _____

4. Is the partnership operating under a trade name? _____

5. Can the partnership be dissolved before the end of five years by mutual agreement of the two partners?

   _____

# CONTINUING PROJECT
## Chapter 5 Activities

New owners often start a business without carefully considering other possible forms of ownership. In this chapter, you will evaluate the advantages and disadvantages of the proprietorship and partnership forms of ownership for a new business.

### Data Collection

1. Review copies of magazines that are written for entrepreneurs. Identify the current issues and problems faced by individual business owners as well as the successful operating procedures described in the magazines.

2. Speak with a banker about the importance of business plans for new businesses. Ask the banker to describe the elements he/she looks for in an effective business plan.

3. Obtain a sample copy of a partnership agreement. Use the sample to develop a partnership agreement for your business. You have found a partner who wants to invest $3,000 and become involved in the operation of the business. After you have completed the agreement, ask your teacher, a business person, or a lawyer to review it with you.

### Analysis

1. Develop a chart that compares the proprietorship and partnership forms of business ownership for your business. Be certain to consider financial, personal, and management factors. When you have finished the analysis, decide whether you will remain a sole proprietor or whether you will form a partnership. Then begin the process of identifying and preparing the necessary documents to organize the ownership of your business.

2. Develop an outline for a business plan for your new business. Begin to list the information that will go into each section of the plan. Identify the information you need to complete the business plan and the sources of that information. Continue to develop the business plan during the time you are working on this Continuing Project.

# Study Guide

**Part A**—*Directions:* Indicate your answer to each of the following questions by circling either yes or no in the Answers column.

| | | Answers | For Scoring |
|---|---|---|---|
| 1. | Do knowledge workers prepare detailed instructions that direct computers to perform specific tasks? | yes no | 1. _____ |
| 2. | Are data prepared after information has been gathered? | yes no | 2. _____ |
| 3. | Was the first computer, called the ENIAC, developed in 1965? | yes no | 3. _____ |
| 4. | Does applications software serve the general purpose of operating computer hardware? | yes no | 4. _____ |
| 5. | Is it possible to send and receive information from other computers by using a communications application software program? | yes no | 5. _____ |
| 6. | Is a microcomputer smaller than a minicomputer? | yes no | 6. _____ |
| 7. | Is the major disadvantage of word processing software that entire documents must be rekeyed when changes are made? | yes no | 7. _____ |
| 8. | With a special type of monitor, is it possible to manipulate data by merely touching a monitor's screen with your finger? | yes no | 8. _____ |
| 9. | Are voice input devices used widely? | yes no | 9. _____ |
| 10. | Is multitasking unproductive because of the wait time between tasks? | yes no | 10. _____ |
| 11. | Can information from different computer systems be shared with branch office computers located in other countries? | yes no | 11. _____ |
| 12. | Does E-mail make it possible to send a copy of a document from one location to another over telephone lines? | yes no | 12. _____ |
| 13. | Has the fiber optic cable made the information superhighway possible? | yes no | 13. _____ |
| 14. | Have computers eliminated routine jobs calling for few skills and little knowledge? | yes no | 14. _____ |
| 15. | Should managers be concerned about employees who become unhappy about job changes when new equipment is installed? | yes no | 15. _____ |
| 16. | Do ergonomic experts study the relationships between people and the machines they use? | yes no | 16. _____ |
| 17. | Is an integrated information system an organized way to capture, store, retrieve, and distribute information for decision-making purposes? | yes no | 17. _____ |
| 18. | In developing any type of integrated information system, are cost and quality two of the most significant factors? | yes no | 18. _____ |
| 19. | Is information processing costly when a computerized or traditional system is used? | yes no | 19. _____ |
| 20. | When developing an integrated information system, is it necessary to know the specific information needs of managers? | yes no | 20. _____ |

**Part B**—*Directions:* For each of the following statements, select the word, or group of words, that best completes the statement. In the Answers column, write the letter corresponding to the answer selected.

| | Answers | For Scoring |
|---|---|---|

1. Which of the following items is NOT computer hardware? (a) CPU, (b) chip, (c) keyboard, (d) GUI. ............................................................ _____ 1. _____

2. Which of the following is NOT a storage device for processed data? (a) floppy disk, (b) mouse, (c) magnetic tape, (d) optical disk. ......................... _____ 2. _____

3. Software programs that prepare financial statements and calculate what the profit might have been under different conditions are (a) database programs (b) utilities, (c) tutorials, (d) spreadsheets. ............................................ _____ 3. _____

4. A large disk that uses a laser beam to scan, record, and play back all images appearing on documents, including graphics, is (a) a hard disk, (b) a terminal, (c) an optical disk, (d) a videodisc. ......................................... _____ 4. _____

5. In what type of system can recorded telephone calls be saved temporarily, listened to several times, and transferred to another person? (a) management information system, (b) E-mail system, (c) multimedia system, (d) voice messaging system. ................................................................................. _____ 5. _____

6. The letters used to describe the connecting of many types of computers so that messages from one end user can be sent to others in a building is (a) LAN, (b) DPS, (c) MIS, (d) DSS. ................................................ _____ 6. _____

7. When introducing new equipment, which principle should NOT be followed? (a) Notify workers well in advance of changes. (b) Explain how activities will be performed more efficiently. (c) Introduce changes quickly. (d) Provide training. _____ 7. _____

8. What impact does moving from a traditional office to a fully automated office have on the nature of jobs? (a) Jobs change quite a bit. (b) Jobs change, but only to a small degree. (c) Jobs stay the same, but the work is done more quickly. (d) Morale improves quickly. ............................................................ _____ 8. _____

9. What type of system provides information for managing and controlling internal operations of a business? (a) operational information, (b) management information, (c) decision support, (d) computer information. ....................... _____ 9. _____

10. When developing an IIS, which of the following steps should NOT be followed? (a) Appoint a director who appoints project teams. (b) Put the IIS into operation gradually while the existing system continues. (c) Make no changes once the system is started. (d) Install and test the hardware and software. ...... _____ 10. _____

**Part C**—*Directions:* For each numbered item, indicate by a check mark in the appropriate column whether it is classified as computer input, output, or processing.

| | Input | Output | Processing | For Scoring |
|---|---|---|---|---|
| 1. Keyboard .................................... | | | | 1. _____ |
| 2. Track ball .................................. | | | | 2. _____ |
| 3. Printer ..................................... | | | | 3. _____ |
| 4. Multitasking ............................... | | | | 4. _____ |
| 5. Scanner .................................... | | | | 5. _____ |

**Directions:** Study each controversial issue carefully. Follow the advice of your teacher before listing in the columns provided reasons why people might answer Yes or No. Your teacher may want you to work with a classmate, talk with others in your community to gather information, or use the library to gather facts.

8-1. Is it likely that by the year 2005, there will be plenty of jobs in which people will not need to know how to use a computer?

| Reasons for "Yes" | Reasons for "No" |
| --- | --- |
|  |  |

8-2.   Has the extensive use of computers by businesses caused more jobs to be lost than to be gained?

| Reasons for "Yes" | Reasons for "No" |
| --- | --- |
|  |  |

# PROBLEMS

**8-A.** Check whether the items listed below are more often associated with a traditional office or an electronic office.

| Item | Traditional Office | Electronic Office |
|------|:---:|:---:|
| 1. Filing cabinets | _____ | _____ |
| 2. Modem | _____ | _____ |
| 3. Facsimile machine | _____ | _____ |
| 4. Typewriter | _____ | _____ |
| 5. Cellular phone | _____ | _____ |
| 6. Stenographer | _____ | _____ |
| 7. Office messenger | _____ | _____ |
| 8. Laser printer | _____ | _____ |

**8-B.** Below is a sketch of a computer system. In the blank lines provided, write in the names of the component parts.

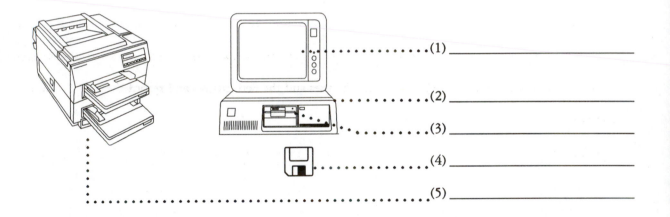

(1) _____

(2) _____

(3) _____

(4) _____

(5) _____

**8-C.** After each task described, write the name of the type of computer software needed to perform each task.

1. Key a letter or other business document. _____

2. Create a newsletter for the business. _____

3. Prepare accounting financial statements. _____

4. Develop a bar or pie chart. _____

5. Store a variety of information about all employees in a business. _____

6. A program to make it easy to use and manage your software. _____

**8-D.** Small handheld computers called personal digital assistants (PDAs) are devices the size of a thin book and contain a special pen that can be used for such purposes as writing messages on the machine—or punching in messages using a miniature keyboard—and sending or receiving fax messages. They are also used as calendars for scheduling, and other routine tasks. Study the figures below from a survey that shows how business owners use their PDAs. Then answer the questions that follow.

|  |  | **Owners** | **Students** |
|---|---|---|---|
| a. | Keep telephone numbers and addresses | 78.9% | _____ |
| b. | Calendar scheduling functions | 73.7 | _____ |
| c. | Send and receive electronic mail | 31.6 | _____ |
| d. | Take notes using its pen input device | 21.1 | _____ |
| e. | Send and receive faxes | 10.5 | _____ |

1. Which two uses would you most often select if you owned a PDA? _____

_____

_____

2. With permission of your teacher, poll your classmates to find the two uses each student would most often

   select if he or she owned a PDA. Calculate the uses and the percentages and record them in the column

   above.

3. What conclusions can you draw when you compare answers from your class and those from the survey?

_____

_____

_____

_____

**8-E.** Inputting data into computers may be done by using any of the following devices: keyboard, scanner, mouse, pen, and voice. For each question below, write in the device that best applies to each situation.

1. Which input device is most used by the greatest number of people? _____

2. Which device would efficiently convert to disks many typed documents stored in file cabinets?

_____

3. Which device do office workers prefer to use in addition to a keyboard? _____

4. Which device do many executives prefer? _____

5. Which device has experienced the most difficulty in correctly inputting data?

_____

**8-F.** For each item listed, indicate whether it is a part of telecommunications.

|   |   | Yes | No |
|---|---|---|---|
| 1. | An airmail letter sent to Argentina. ..................................................... | ____ | ____ |
| 2. | A message sent via a microcomputer from one floor in a building to a microcomputer located on another floor in the same building. .......................... | ____ | ____ |
| 3. | A chart sent by facsimile from Chicago to Houston. ................................ | ____ | ____ |
| 4. | A message sent from a computer operator in Atlanta to a computer operator in Toronto, Canada. ..................................................................................... | ____ | ____ |
| 5. | A telephone message to a manager in another city was left with the receptionist because the extension was busy. .................................................................... | ____ | ____ |

**8-G.** Study the cost of installing a new computer system from the information provided. Then answer the following questions:

|   | Cost | Percent |
|---|---|---|
| 1 Minicomputer | $15,000 | _____ |
| 10 Desktop computers | 12,000 | _____ |
| 2 Laser printers | 4,600 | _____ |
| 8 Software programs | 3,200 | _____ |
| Installation | 3,800 | _____ |
| Training for employees | 5,200 | _____ |
| Total | _____ | _____ |

1. In the column shown above, write the total cost of the computer system.

2. In the column provided, calculate the percentage cost of each component of the system.

3. To what activity should most of the training time be devoted? _____

    _____

4. What is the total cost of the various pieces of hardware?  **$** _____

5. What percent of the total cost is for hardware and what percent is for other costs?

    a. Hardware _____

    b. Other Costs _____

6. What other major costs are not shown? _____

    _____

    _____

    _____

    _____

8-H. Bowman Brothers has a computer installation. The company has four personal computers located in different office areas which are tied into a larger computer system. The areas are listed below by function. You are to write in the spaces provided some of the ways the PCs could be used in each area.

1.  Personnel Department

    a. _____

    b. _____

    c. _____

2.  Sales Department

    a. _____

    b. _____

    c. _____

3.  Inventory Control, Purchasing Department

    a. _____

    b. _____

    c. _____

8-I. Indicate how multimedia with a computer might improve each of the following management problems.

1.  A district manager must train eight salespeople to demonstrate and sell a new product to customers. The salespeople are always traveling.

    _____

    _____

    _____

2.  A group of five very busy branch managers located in different countries need to meet as soon as possible to discuss an explosion at one of the branches. The meeting must occur within two hours so that a plan can be made that will prevent similar accidents at other branches.

    _____

    _____

    _____

    _____

    _____

8-J. Check the appropriate column to indicate which computer information system would provide the needed information for each item listed below.

| | Decision Support System | Management Information System | Operational Information System |
|---|---|---|---|
| 1. Total sales for the day from each of the eight point-of-sale terminals. | ▬ | ____ | ____ |
| 2. Yearly total sales compared to other major competitors. | ____ | ____ | ____ |
| 3. A breakdown of manufacturing costs for every quarter of the year. | ____ | ____ | ____ |
| 4. Total hours worked for each assembly line worker for the last three weeks. | ____ | ____ | ____ |
| 5. A forecast of sales for the next three years. | ____ | ____ | ____ |
| 6. Total cost of goods sold and operating expenses for each month during the past year. | ____ | ____ | ____ |

8-K. Assume that during the next 18 months, a new inexpensive device will become available that will enable office workers to enter voice messages (words and numbers) into computers with 99 percent accuracy. What problems might managers who buy these devices for their workers have to solve?

1. The task of keying data into computers using keyboards will no longer be necessary; consequently, some

   workers will no longer be needed.

   _____

   _____

   _____

   _____

2. Many jobs involving some keying of data will need to be redesigned.

   _____

   _____

   _____

   _____

# CONTINUING PROJECT
## Chapter 8 Activities

It is easy for a new business owner to ignore the need for an organized information management system. Problems occur if business records and other information are not kept or are poorly organized. Not only will time be wasted searching for information, but needed information can actually be lost. The owner of the business will spend a great deal of time dealing with information. In this chapter, you will review information management systems for small businesses and determine the advantages of developing a computer-based system.

### Data Collection

1. Interview an owner of a small business. Discuss the type of information management system used. Identify (1) the type of records and information maintained, (2) whether the system is manual or automated, (3) who is responsible for information management, and (4) how the system could be improved.

2. Visit a computer systems retailer and discuss the hardware and software the retailer recommends for new small businesses. Collect information on system prices, capabilities, and ease of operation.

3. Study the Yellow Pages of a telephone directory to identify businesses that offer information management services for businesses. Call one company and determine the types of services offered and prices charged for those services.

### Analysis

1. A set of records will be needed for your business in order to manage purchasing and inventory. Describe the basic system you will use to receive merchandise, pay invoices, maintain an accurate record of inventory, and record daily sales for each product.

2. Identify several information management programs that can be used on a microcomputer to accomplish the tasks listed in Step 1 above. Compare the features and prices of the programs and identify the one that you believe is most appropriate for your business.

# Study Guide

**Part A**—*Directions:* Indicate your answer to each of the following questions by circling either yes or no in the Answers column.

|  | | Answers | For Scoring |
| --- | --- | --- | --- |

1. Does communication include the passing of factual data rather than the sharing of ideas, beliefs, and opinions? ............................................................ yes no 1. _____
2. Does information overload lead to effective decision making? ...................... yes no 2. _____
3. Is a business chart or diagram a type of nonverbal communication? ............. yes no 3. _____
4. Do nonverbal messages always confirm verbal messages? ............................ yes no 4. _____
5. In an open communication system, are creativity and problem solving encouraged at all levels? .................................................................................... yes no 5. _____
6. While some organizations distrust employees and encourage secrecy, do other organizations trust employees and encourage information sharing? ................ yes no 6. _____
7. Do all employees usually prefer a corporate culture with an open communication system? ........................................................................................................ yes no 7. _____
8. Does certain information, such as budget allocations, usually flow upward from lower-level managers to top-level managers? .................................................. yes no 8. _____
9. Do lower-level managers usually rely on upper-level managers for information about the quality of employee performance? ................................................... yes no 9. _____
10. When people hear you, do they always understand what you are saying? ....... yes no 10. _____
11. Is upward communication more likely to be distorted in closed, rather than in open, corporate cultures? ............................................................................... yes no 11. _____
12. Are lateral communications more likely to exist in open, rather than in closed, corporate cultures? ........................................................................................... yes no 12. _____
13. Has it been estimated that 80 percent of poor management decisions occur because of ineffective communications? ........................................................ yes no 13. _____
14. Since informal groups have little or no influence over the behavior of individual workers, should managers ignore informal groups? .......................................... yes no 14. _____
15. Generally, should managers interfere with grapevines? ................................. yes no 15. _____
16. Is a compromise strategy the best way to handle most conflict situations? ...... yes no 16. _____
17. When participants face one another in meetings, is communication discouraged? ............................................................................................................... yes no 17. _____
18. Although Americans, Australians, and the British all speak English, do language problems exist among the countries? ................................................... yes no 18. _____
19. Because it is time consuming, are managers who consciously engage in two-way communications usually less successful than those who do not? .............. yes no 19. _____
20. Do employees who are informed about their companies have stronger positive feelings than those who are not? ...................................................................... yes no 20. _____

**Part B**—*Directions:* For each of the following statements, select the word, or group of words, that best completes the statement. In the Answers column, write the letter corresponding to the answer selected.

|  | Answers | For Scoring |
|---|---|---|

1. On average, what portion of a day do managers spend communicating? (a) 1/4, (b) 1/2, (c) 2/3, (d) 3/4 .................................................... _____ 1. _____

2. Employees who tell supervisors about machine breakdowns, but do not admit to failing to oil machines according to a schedule, are guilty of information (a) breakdowns, (b) distractions, (c) distortions, (d) networks. ......................... _____ 2. _____

3. When creativity and problem solving are encouraged at all levels and trust and supportiveness exist to a high degree in an organization, what type of communication system exists? (a) open, (b) upward, (c) downward, (d) closed. .......... _____ 3. _____

4. When conflicts are relatively unimportant, which strategy should managers use? (a) avoidance, (b) compromise, (c) win-lose, (d) interference. .................. _____ 4. _____

5. How does the NGT differ from a regular meeting of workers involved in solving a problem? (a) The NGT requires everyone to agree to the solution. (b) The NGT requires open voting. (c) The NGT requires all members to offer solutions. (d) The NGT forces the manager to select the solution. ......,.............. _____ 5. _____

6. Which is NOT a good suggestion for running effective meetings? (a) Decide who should and should not attend the meeting. (b) Stick to a specific agenda. (c) Schedule the meeting at the manager's convenience. (d) Arrange seating so that participants face one another. ........................................... _____ 6. _____

7. Management by Walking Around was designed to help which communication problem? (a) loud and unpredictive workers, (b) errors passed through the grapevine, (c) employee conflicts, (d) upward communications. ........................... _____ 7. _____

8. The following are all good rules for listening. Which is the most basic rule? (a) Put the person at ease. (b) Stop talking. (c) Remove distractions. (d) Ask questions. ................................................................................. _____ 8. _____

9. If a manager needs to reprimand an employee, which communication channel is best to use? (a) group meeting, (b) oral, (c) written, (d) formal. ..........,......... _____ 9. _____

10. The best way to deliver a compliment to an employee for excellent work is (a) orally to personalize it, (b) in writing in order to record it, (c) both orally and in writing, (d) orally in a private meeting. ......,............................................. _____ 10. _____

**Part C**—*Directions:* In the Answers column, write the letter of the word or expression in Column I that most closely matches each statement in Column II.

| Column I | Column II | Answers | For Scoring |
|---|---|---|---|
| A. Brainstorming | 1. Develops when interfering with the achievement of another person's goals. ........,........ ,.. | _____ | 1. _____ |
| B. Closed culture | | | |
| C. Communication | 2. Someone slams a door. ,.............. ...,............. | _____ | 2. _____ |
| D. Conflict | 3. Sharing ideas, beliefs, and opinions. ..........,... | _____ | 3. _____ |
| E. Culture | 4. How people consciously or unconsciously change messages ,......................................... | _____ | |
| F. Distortion | | | |
| G. Distraction | 5. A discussion technique that stimulates ideas. | _____ | |
| H. Grapevine | | | |

# Study Guide

**Part A**—*Directions:* Indicate your answer to each of the following questions by circling either yes or no in the Answers column.

|  | | Answers | For Scoring |
|---|---|---|---|
| 1. | Does communication include the passing of factual data rather than the sharing of ideas, beliefs, and opinions? ................................................................ | yes   no | 1. _____ |
| 2. | Does information overload lead to effective decision making? ....................... | yes   no | 2. _____ |
| 3. | Is a business chart or diagram a type of nonverbal communication? .............. | yes   no | 3. _____ |
| 4. | Do nonverbal messages always confirm verbal messages? ............................ | yes   no | 4. _____ |
| 5. | In an open communication system, are creativity and problem solving encouraged at all levels? ................................................................................ | yes   no | 5. _____ |
| 6. | While some organizations distrust employees and encourage secrecy, do other organizations trust employees and encourage information sharing? ................ | yes   no | 6. _____ |
| 7. | Do all employees usually prefer a corporate culture with an open communication system? ................................................................................................ | yes   no | 7. _____ |
| 8. | Does certain information, such as budget allocations, usually flow upward from lower-level managers to top-level managers? ............................................. | yes   no | 8. _____ |
| 9. | Do lower-level managers usually rely on upper-level managers for information about the quality of employee performance? ............................................... | yes   no | 9. _____ |
| 10. | When people hear you, do they always understand what you are saying? ....... | yes   no | 10. _____ |
| 11. | Is upward communication more likely to be distorted in closed, rather than in open, corporate cultures? ......................................................................... | yes   no | 11. _____ |
| 12. | Are lateral communications more likely to exist in open, rather than in closed, corporate cultures? ................................................................................... | yes   no | 12. _____ |
| 13. | Has it been estimated that 80 percent of poor management decisions occur because of ineffective communications? ................................................... | yes   no | 13. _____ |
| 14. | Since informal groups have little or no influence over the behavior of individual workers, should managers ignore informal groups? ...................................... | yes   no | 14. _____ |
| 15. | Generally, should managers interfere with grapevines? ................................ | yes   no | 15. _____ |
| 16. | Is a compromise strategy the best way to handle most conflict situations? ...... | yes   no | 16. _____ |
| 17. | When participants face one another in meetings, is communication discouraged? ....................................................................................................... | yes   no | 17. _____ |
| 18. | Although Americans, Australians, and the British all speak English, do language problems exist among the countries? ............................................... | yes   no | 18. _____ |
| 19. | Because it is time consuming, are managers who consciously engage in two-way communications usually less successful than those who do not? .............. | yes   no | 19. _____ |
| 20. | Do employees who are informed about their companies have stronger positive feelings than those who are not? ................................................................ | yes   no | 20. _____ |

| | Answers | For Scoring |
|---|---|---|
| 1. On average, what portion of a day do managers spend communicating? (a) 1/4, (b) 1/2, (c) 2/3, (d) 3/4 ................ | _____ | 1. _____ |
| 2. Employees who tell supervisors about machine breakdowns, but do not admit to failing to oil machines according to a schedule, are guilty of information (a) breakdowns, (b) distractions, (c) distortions, (d) networks. .......... | _____ | 2. _____ |
| 3. When creativity and problem solving are encouraged at all levels and trust and supportiveness exist to a high degree in an organization, what type of communication system exists? (a) open, (b) upward, (c) downward, (d) closed. .......... | _____ | 3. _____ |
| 4. When conflicts are relatively unimportant, which strategy should managers use? (a) avoidance, (b) compromise, (c) win-lose, (d) interference. .......... | _____ | 4. _____ |
| 5. How does the NGT differ from a regular meeting of workers involved in solving a problem? (a) The NGT requires everyone to agree to the solution. (b) The NGT requires open voting. (c) The NGT requires all members to offer solutions. (d) The NGT forces the manager to select the solution. .......... | _____ | 5. _____ |
| 6. Which is NOT a good suggestion for running effective meetings? (a) Decide who should and should not attend the meeting. (b) Stick to a specific agenda. (c) Schedule the meeting at the manager's convenience. (d) Arrange seating so that participants face one another. .......... | _____ | 6. _____ |
| 7. Management by Walking Around was designed to help which communication problem? (a) loud and unproductive workers, (b) errors passed through the grapevine, (c) employee conflicts, (d) upward communications. .......... | _____ | 7. _____ |
| 8. The following are all good rules for listening. Which is the most basic rule? (a) Put the person at ease. (b) Stop talking. (c) Remove distractions. (d) Ask questions. .......... | _____ | 8. _____ |
| 9. If a manager needs to reprimand an employee, which communication channel is best to use? (a) group meeting, (b) oral, (c) written, (d) formal. .......... | _____ | 9. _____ |
| 10. The best way to deliver a compliment to an employee for excellent work is (a) orally to personalize it, (b) in writing in order to record it, (c) both orally and in writing, (d) orally in a private meeting. .......... | _____ | 10. _____ |

**Part C**—*Directions:* In the Answers column, write the letter of the word or expression in Column I that most closely matches each statement in Column II.

| Column I | Column II | Answers | For Scoring |
|---|---|---|---|
| A. Brainstorming | 1. Develops when interfering with the achievement of another person's goals. .......... | _____ | 1. _____ |
| B. Closed culture | 2. Someone slams a door. .......... | _____ | 2. _____ |
| C. Communication | 3. Sharing ideas, beliefs, and opinions. .......... | _____ | 3. _____ |
| D. Conflict | 4. How people consciously or unconsciously change messages. .......... | _____ | 4. _____ |
| E. Culture | 5. A discussion technique that stimulates ideas. .......... | _____ | 5. _____ |
| F. Distortion | | | |
| G. Distraction | | | |
| H. Grapevine | | | |

**Directions:** Study each controversial issue carefully. Follow the advice of your teacher before listing in the columns provided reasons why people might answer Yes or No. Your teacher may want you to work with a classmate, talk with others in your community to gather information, or use the library to gather facts.

9-1. Is writing relatively unimportant in business considering that the average executive spends only about 30 minutes each day writing and numerous hours of time communicating orally?

| Reasons for "Yes" | Reasons for "No" |
| --- | --- |
|  |  |

9-2. Should most meetings be limited to 30 minutes because so much valuable work time is lost talking about trivial business and nonbusiness matters?

| Reasons for "Yes" | Reasons for "No" |
| --- | --- |
|  |  |

# PROBLEMS

**9-A.** Check whether each of the following situations describing a barrier to communication is a distraction or a distortion.

|  |  | Distraction | Distortion |
|---|---|---|---|
| 1. | During a meeting, a worker throws a wad of paper into a wastebasket located across the room. | _____ | _____ |
| 2. | A lawyer's beeper beeps during a conversation with a client. | _____ | _____ |
| 3. | When the receptionist told her manager he had a call, she neglected to say that the call was from the doctor who had just completed major surgery on the manager's wife. | _____ | _____ |
| 4. | A client's name was misspelled on an otherwise well-written message. | _____ | _____ |
| 5. | Telephone calls constantly interrupted the manager, who was composing an important report. | _____ | _____ |
| 6. | A supervisor had a serious problem with an employee. When reporting to the manager, the supervisor merely said, "One of my employees has a small problem, but I'm sure it can be worked out." | _____ | _____ |
| 7. | "Skip the minor details, Cindy. What are the important points?" | _____ | _____ |
| 8. | "At today's meeting, please don't mention that some of the gang was smoking again because written warnings or pink slips will be issued. Instead, let's ask for a discussion of the importance of not smoking in the plant." | _____ | _____ |

**9-B.** For each of the following communication situations, identify (1) the sender (2) the receiver, and (3) the message channel.

1. A customer calls the service manager of an auto-repair shop to make an appointment to have her car repaired.

    a. sender _____

    b. receiver _____

    c. message channel _____

2. A sales manager sends a memo to the head of the accounting department requesting a report on customers who have not paid their balances owed.

    a. sender _____

    b. receiver _____

    c. message channel _____

3. While they are working, Jack tells Colleen about a rumor that some other employees might get an increase in pay next month.

    a. sender _____

    b. receiver _____

    c. message channel _____

4. The branch manager of the Redbank National Bank sends Harvey Kwolek a computerized form letter to inform him that his checking account is overdrawn.

    a. sender _____

    b. receiver _____

    c. message channel _____

9-C. Shown below are the costs in a recent year of two methods to prepare a one-page business letter of average length that is transcribed on a personal computer. Study both methods and answer the following questions in the space provided.

| | Face-to-Face Dictation | Machine Dictation | Difference |
|---|---|---|---|
| Dictator's time | $6.55 | $6.55 | _____ |
| Secretary's time | 6.26 | 2.35 | _____ |
| Non-productive labor | 1.93 | 1.34 | _____ |
| Fixed charges | 3.20 | 2.24 | _____ |
| Materials | .34 | .34 | _____ |
| Postage | .29 | .29 | _____ |
| Total | $_____ | $_____ | _____ |

1. Calculate the total cost to dictate to a secretary in a face-to-face situation. Record your answer above.

2. Calculate the total cost when using dictation equipment. Record your answer above.

3. Calculate the difference in cost for each item. Record your answers above.

4. Why might both the dictator's and secretary's time be greater in face-to-face dictation?

_____

_____

_____

5. What percent of the total cost of a letter dictated into a machine is devoted to labor costs? _____

6. How much more per letter does a business spend in face-to-face dictation?_____

9-D. By checking the appropriate column, indicate whether the nonverbal message confirms or contradicts the verbal message.

| | Verbal Message | Nonverbal Message | Confirms | Contradicts |
|---|---|---|---|---|
| 1. | "Please sit and listen, students." | Snaps fingers. | _____ | _____ |
| 2. | "I'll wait patiently for another five minutes." | Taps fingers on the desk. | _____ | _____ |
| 3. | "Sure. I'll be happy to work on that project." | Turns eyes toward window and drops voice. | _____ | _____ |
| 4. | "I'm thinking... I'm thinking." | Looks downward and places finger over lips. | _____ | _____ |
| 5. | "I'm interested in your ideas." | Leans toward person with steady eye contact. | _____ | _____ |

9-E. Place a check mark in one of the two columns on the right for each item below that describes a characteristic within an organization.

|  | Corporate Culture | |
| --- | --- | --- |
|  | Open | Closed |
| 1. Employees call their bosses by their first names and eat in the same cafeteria. ........ | _____ | _____ |
| 2. Employees may send their gripes using E-mail directly to upper-level managers, who respond quickly. ...................................... | _____ | _____ |
| 3. All contact about business matters must be done through formal appointments, at meetings, or by memos. ................................ | _____ | _____ |
| 4. Informal communication methods are discouraged and most messages flow downward. .................................................. | _____ | _____ |
| 5. Self-directed work teams were introduced but failed because most managers would not surrender authority. ...................................... | _____ | _____ |

9-F. How do you handle conflict situations? Place a "1" in the column that represents your preferred strategy and a "2" in the column that represents your second-choice strategy. Discuss answers with your classmates to compare similarities and differences.

| Conflict Situations | Strategies | | |
| --- | --- | --- | --- |
|  | Avoid | Compromise | Win/Lose |
| 1. An office mate who is a good friend wants to take her daily mid-morning break with you at 10:00 a.m., but another friend definitely prefers 10:30. ........................................ | _____ | _____ | _____ |
| 2. Two other managers cannot agree on what amount should be budgeted for hiring a part-time worker who will help all three of you. They turn to you for support. ........................... | _____ | _____ | _____ |
| 3. Two co-workers are moving with you to a new office area. Both want the larger desk that overlooks a courtyard. Although you work well with one co-worker, you do not get along with the other. However, you also want the desk that overlooks the courtyard. ........................................ | _____ | _____ | _____ |
| 4. Your sales manager promised an added cash award to the person with the highest weekly sales. You and five other salespeople want to win the award. ........................................ | _____ | _____ | _____ |
| 5. A newly hired worker was just promoted. Because you had worked longer and harder, you complained bitterly to your supervisor and accused him of showing favoritism. You storm out of the office and must decide what to do. ........................................ | _____ | _____ | _____ |

9-G. Translate the following two messages by placing the American English word or words on the blank line after the British English.

1. "A *barrister* _____ was struck at a *roundabout* _____. Her *bonnet* _____ and *boot* _____ were badly damaged. And *petrol* _____ was leaking onto the *pavement* _____.

2. The pay *rise* _____ that was promised the *black coated* _____ workers was cancelled just before they left for the day to catch the *tube* _____.

9-H. A new president for a business that has problems just hired you as its communications expert. As your first task, the president wants to know how you would handle the following situations, which have occurred regularly over the past several months. Provide two suggestions for each situation.

1. "Whenever a problem arises, everyone has a solution, but no one does anything because everyone talks and no one listens."

   a. _____

   b. _____

2. "I never know whether to chew someone out on the phone, in person, or by memo. Of course, the same question applies to praising a good worker or informing workers of new policies."

   a. _____

   b. _____

3. "My managers seem great at communicating down to others, but not enough information flows upward."

   a. _____

   b. _____

4. "Our workers don't talk to their managers enough. They do their jobs, but often there are errors because they don't understand the instructions. Not even the managers talk to one another enough."

   a. _____

   b. _____

9-I. Read each of the communications situations described below. For each situation, indicate whether oral or written communications will be more effective by checking the appropriate column.

| Situation | Type of Communication | |
| --- | --- | --- |
| | Written | Oral |
| 1. A manager wants to tell a few employees how to use a new cash register. ............. | _____ | _____ |
| 2. An employee wants to tell the company president about a more efficient way to unload merchandise from trucks. ................................................................. | _____ | _____ |
| 3. A committee chairperson wants to describe a new assignment to committee members. ........................................................................................ | _____ | _____ |
| 4. A sales manager needs to give all salespeople a new set of list prices for products. | _____ | _____ |
| 5. A worker wants to tell another worker her opinion of the new manager. ............. | _____ | _____ |
| 6. The president of a corporation wants to summarize the year's activities of the company for the stockholders. ................................................................. | _____ | _____ |
| 7. A group leader wants the group to determine several ways to solve a problem. ...... | _____ | _____ |
| 8. A large company wants all employees to know about several recent promotions. .. | _____ | _____ |

# CONTINUING PROJECT
## Chapter 9 Activities

As a small business owner, you will be responsible for most if not all communications from your business. Errors in communications or poor communications can be very damaging to a new business as you establish contact with suppliers, other businesses, and customers.

### Data Collection

1. Using newspapers and business magazines, identify situations where businesses faced problems resulting from poor communications. What are the types of communications problems businesses typically have with (1) suppliers, (2) other businesses, and (3) customers?
2. Advertising is one method of communicating with customers. Review the ads of several small businesses to determine the strengths and weaknesses of the communications.

### Analysis

1. Compose a letter that could be sent to the manager of a local park, swimming pool, or sports stadium. Request that your business be given exclusive rights to sell food at that location for a specific period of time.
2. You have been asked by the local organization of retailers to make a brief presentation at their monthly luncheon meeting about your new business. Prepare a five-minute speech that describes the business and its operations and some of the challenges you believe that you will face. (You may want to have some visual aids to use during your speech.) Audio or video tape your speech.

**Directions:** Study each controversial issue carefully. Follow the advice of your teacher before listing in the columns provided reasons why people might answer Yes or No. Your teacher may want you to work with a classmate, talk with others in your community to gather information, or use the library to gather facts.

10-1. Does marketing cause people to purchase products and services they really don't want or need?

| Reasons for "Yes" | Reasons for "No" |
|---|---|
|  |  |

10-2. Are most businesses today customer-oriented?

| Reasons for "Yes" | Reasons for "No" |
|---|---|
|  |  |

# PROBLEMS

10-A. Marketing-oriented firms attempt to identify target markets before they sell their products. For most products, there will be several groups of potential customers. Each group will have different needs and will want a different marketing mix.

For each of the products listed below, describe two unique target markets for the product. Then describe the marketing mix that would be needed to satisfy each of the target markets.

| Product | Description of Target Market | Description of Marketing Mix |
|---|---|---|
| Automobile | #1 | #1 |
| | #2 | #2 |
| Motel | #1 | #1 |
| | #2 | #2 |

# Study Guide

**Part A**—*Directions:* Indicate your answer to each of the following questions by circling either yes or no in the Answers column.

| | | Answers | For Scoring |
|---|---|---|---|

1. Do U. S. consumers have a very limited number of products and services to satisfy their needs? ............................................................... yes no 1. _____

2. Is it possible for companies to spend several million dollars to develop and manufacture one new product? ..................................................... yes no 2. _____

3. Do nearly 90 percent of new products developed by businesses survive in the market for at least five years? ............................................. yes no 3. _____

4. Are most of the products you will be using in ten years currently for sale on the market? .......................................................................... yes no 4. _____

5. Should companies rely on scientists and engineers for their new product ideas? yes no 5. _____

6. Is the amount of money U. S. businesses spend on new product research declining from past years? ................................................................. yes no 6. _____

7. Is research that is done without a specific product in mind known as pure research? .............................................................................. yes no 7. _____

8. Would the redesign of refrigerators and air conditioners to eliminate the use of environmentally damaging chemicals be an example of applied research? ...... yes no 8. _____

9. Do advertising and market research mean the same thing? ......................... yes no 9. _____

10. Should research and testing on new products be conducted before the product is produced and marketed? ............................................................... yes no 10. _____

11. Is manufacturing a special form of production that turns raw and semifinished materials into finished products? ..................................................... yes no 11. _____

12. Does manufacturing require the use of assembly lines and mass production? .. yes no 12. _____

13. Is the conversion of iron ore into steel an example of continuous processing? .. yes no 13. _____

14. Should a company that uses a large quantity of raw materials attempt to locate close to the source of those materials? ............................................... yes no 14. _____

15. Do some cities offer reduced tax rates or even remove some taxes in order to encourage new businesses to locate there? ........................................... yes no 15. _____

16. Are the three important activities that are a part of production planning inventory management, human resource planning, and production scheduling? ..... yes no 16. _____

17. Have the quality management ideas of Dr. W. Edwards Deming failed to improve the competitiveness of U. S. businesses? ......................................... yes no 17. _____

18. Have service businesses grown at a slower rate than manufacturing businesses? yes no 18. _____

19. Does the quality of a service usually depend on who provides the service? ...... yes no 19. _____

20. Are the characteristics of services easier to communicate to customers than the characteristics of products? ........................................................... yes no 20. _____

**Part B**—*Directions:* For each of the following statements, select the word, or group of words, that best completes the statement. In the Answers column, write the letter corresponding to the answer selected.

|  | Answers | For Scoring |
|---|---|---|

1. The process of creating or improving a product is known as (a) marketing, (b) pure research, (c) logistics, (d) product development. ................................ _____ 1. _____

2. A consumer panel is made up of people who (a) do not know the company, (b) have worked for the competitor, (c) sell products to the company's customers, (d) have bought or are likely to buy the company's products. ....................... _____ 2. _____

3. Substituting plastics for metal parts in an automobile to reduce weight and improve efficiency is a product design improvement resulting from (a) marketing research, (b) applied research, (c) pure research, (d) advertising research. ... _____ 3. _____

4. Determining why people buy and what influences their decisions is what type of research? (a) market research, (b) pure research, (c) motivation research, (d) advertising research. ................................................................... _____ 4. _____

5. Which of the following businesses would be *least* likely to locate close to the source of raw materials? (a) furniture manufacturer, (b) steel mill, (c) soft drink bottler, (d) all of the businesses listed would need to locate close to sources of raw materials. ................................................................................ _____ 5. _____

6. The American management expert W. Edwards Deming suggested that the most important goal for businesses is (a) reduced costs, (b) competition, (c) effective marketing, (d) quality. ............................................................... _____ 6. _____

7. The United States is changing from the world's leading manufacturing economy to the leading (a) marketing economy, (b) agriculture economy, (c) production economy, (d) service economy. ................................................................. _____ 7. _____

8. Which of the following is an example of a service business? (a) an equipment rental business, (b) an insurance agency, (c) a home cleaning business, (d) all are examples of service businesses. ....................................................... _____ 8. _____

9. A difference between a product and a service is (a) a service is intangible and a product is tangible, (b) a service can be separated from the person supplying it and a product cannot, (c) the quality of a service depends more on who provides it than does a product, (d) a service can be stored or held longer than a product. _____ 9. _____

10. Scheduling fewer lifeguards at a swimming pool during a particularly cool summer is an example of (a) matching supply and demand, (b) matching cost and price, (c) overemphasizing personnel decisions, (d) a poor marketing decision. _____ 10. _____

**Part C**—*Directions:* In the Answers column, write the letter of the word or expression Column I that most closely matches each statement in Column II.

| Column I | Column II | Answers | For Scoring |
|---|---|---|---|
| A. Custom manufacturing | 1. Short production runs to make batches of different products. ............................ | _____ | 1. _____ |
| B. Mass production | 2. A large number of products is produced, each of which is identical to the next. ................. | _____ | 2. _____ |
| C. Continuous processing | 3. Raw materials are converted in long production runs to make them usable. .................... | _____ | 3. _____ |
| D. Repetitive process | 4. The design and building of a product to meet the specific needs of a purchaser. ................. | _____ | 4. _____ |
| E. Intermittent process | 5. Modules are assembled in the same way to produce the finished product. .......................... | _____ | 5. _____ |

**Directions:** Study each controversial issue carefully. Follow the advice of your teacher before listing in the columns provided reasons why people might answer Yes or No. Your teacher may want you to work with a classmate, talk with others in your community to gather information, or use the library to gather facts.

**11-1.** If a company's research discovers a way to build a safer product but the change makes the product much more expensive and difficult to use, should the company produce and market the product?

| Reasons for "Yes" | Reasons for "No" |
| --- | --- |
| | |

**11-2.** If the United States continues to change from a manufacturing economy to a service economy, will wages and the standard of living for most citizens decline?

| Reasons for "Yes" | Reasons for "No" |
| --- | --- |
| | |

# PROBLEMS

**11-A.** One consumer products firm spent $2,300,000 on research in a recent year. Those dollars were divided among several types of research as follows:

| | |
|---|---|
| Market research | 25% |
| Advertising research | 15% |
| Motivation research | 20% |
| Pure research | 5% |
| Applied research | 35% |

1.  If the company's research budget was 6 percent of the total sales for the year, what was the amount of the company's sales? $ _____

2.  Calculate the amount spent on each type of research.

    a.  Market research      $ _____

    b.  Advertising research   $ _____

    c.  Motivation research    $ _____

    d.  Pure research           $ _____

    e.  Applied research       $ _____

3.  In the space below, construct a bar graph that shows the percentage of the total research budget spent on each type of research.

**11-B.** Jackson and Smith, Inc., is considering building a new factory. They have limited the choice of location to three states. One of the factors they are considering is the taxes and fees they will have to pay in each state. They have collected the following information:

| Tax or Fee | State #1 | State #2 | State #3 |
|---|---|---|---|
| Corporate income tax | 3% | 6% | 10% |
| Property tax | $35/1,000 | $30/1,000 | $25/1,000 |
| Annual corporation fee | $1,000 | $0 | $250 |
| Annual license fees | $100 | $1,000 | $3,000 |

If the company plans to build a $6,000,000 plant and estimates a net income the first year of $360,000, compute the total cost of taxes and fees for the first year in each state.

State #1 _____     State #2 _____     State #3 _____

**11-C.** The Raydon Company is planning an important change in one of its products. Management has identified the following steps that need to be completed and the estimated time it will take to complete each step:

| | | |
|---|---|---|
| 1. | Review of old product by consumer panel | 14 days |
| 2. | Developing and testing of product model | 70 days |
| 3. | Marketing research | 40 days |
| 4. | Developing manufacturing facilities | 60 days |
| 5. | Test marketing | 90 days |
| 6. | Production and distribution | 30 days |

The Raydon Company is beginning the process on March 15. Assume that each step must be completed before the next step is started. Identify the date each step will be completed and the earliest date customers will be able to buy the new product.

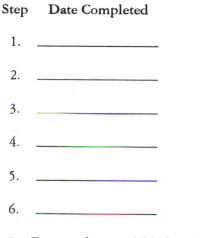

**Step    Date Completed**

1. _____

2. _____

3. _____

4. _____

5. _____

6. _____

7. Date product available for sale _____

**11-D.** You and your friend are planning to start a service business. The business will provide pet and plant care for people while they are on vacation. For each of the following characteristics of service businesses, a customer need is identified. In the column on the right, describe one thing your business will do to ensure that your business will be able to meet that specific customer need.

| Characteristic | Specific Customer Need | What will your business do to meet the customer need? |
|---|---|---|
| 1. Form | Some people have exotic plants requiring special care. | |
| 2. Availability | People want to be certain the promised services are provided so they don't have to worry while on vacation. | |
| 3. Quality | Pet owners want their pets to receive attention and to follow their accustomed schedule. | |
| 4. Timing | Some pet owners need to find a place to leave their pets for an afternoon or evening on very short notice. | |

11-E. Companies regularly work to identify new products that they can introduce to consumers. Those products can result from pure or applied research, from the study of consumer needs, and from the recommendations of customers or company employees. Many new product ideas are developed creatively when business people think about problems and needs.

For each of the categories listed below, identify an existing product that appears to have been developed to fit that category. List that product or its description in the second column. Then in the third column, try to develop a new product idea that fits the criteria.

| Criteria | Current Product | New Product Idea |
|---|---|---|
| 1. Making a household task easier ...... | _____ | _____ |
| 2. A new recreational activity ............ | _____ | _____ |
| 3. A new use for an old product ......... | _____ | _____ |
| 4. A product related to a holiday or a special event ................................. | _____ | _____ |
| 5. A product that uses new technology | _____ | _____ |
| 6. A product that makes it easier to use another product ....................... | _____ | _____ |
| 7. A product designed to reduce the chance of accident or injury ........... | _____ | _____ |

**11-F.** An automobile manufacturer asked a marketing research firm to survey prospective new car buyers. One of the questions asked the respondents to identify the factor that was most important to them when purchasing a new car. The responses are summarized in the following table:

| Factor | Number of Responses | % of Total |
|--------|--------------------|-----------|
| Price | 210 | _____ |
| Styling | 480 | _____ |
| Brand name | 365 | _____ |
| Reputation of dealer | 240 | _____ |
| Special accessories | 245 | _____ |
| Fuel economy | 400 | _____ |
| Other | 60 | _____ |
| Total respondents | _____ | |

1. Complete the table by calculating the total number of people responding to the survey and the percentage of respondents who selected each of the factors as most important.
2. After reviewing the results, make two specific written recommendations to the automobile manufacturer to help in the design of cars for the types of people surveyed.

Recommendation #1

_____

_____

_____

_____

Recommendation #2

_____

_____

_____

_____

# CONTINUING PROJECT
## Chapter 11 Activities

Two important elements of product planning for a new retail business are (1) gathering information from potential customers about their attitudes toward the product and (2) scheduling the activities to be completed in organizing the business. You will complete those two activities in this chapter.

### Data Collection

1.  Identify five people who represent potential customers for your business. They are your consumer panel, so make certain they represent different ages, income levels, occupations, and interests. Schedule a 45-minute meeting with the group. Describe the business to them and ask for their reactions. Have them recommend what they would like to see in the products, prices, and locations. They might also recommend some effective ways to promote the business. After you have met with the panel, write a report that summarizes its recommendations.
2.  Identify at least four sources of research or other information that will be important to you as you plan and manage your business. Provide a brief description of the source and the type of information provided.

### Analysis

1.  Using retailing or small business management textbooks, find a list of the recommended steps for opening a new business. Then develop a schedule that lists the activities in the order that they would be completed for your business. Prepare a time schedule for the completion of each activity. Make certain you allow enough time to complete each activity. Project the date you will be able to open your business.
2.  Since your business relies on effective service, prepare a list of services you will provide to customers. Then prepare a step-by-step procedure for each of the services to ensure that it is provided effectively each time.

**Directions:** Study each controversial issue carefully. Follow the advice of your teacher before listing in the columns provided reasons why people might answer Yes or No. Your teacher may want you to work with a classmate, talk with others in your community to gather information, or use the library to gather facts.

13-1. If a business is facing increasing prices and inflation, should it cut the quality of the products and services sold in order to prevent major increases in the prices they charge to customers?

| Reasons for "Yes" | Reasons for "No" |
|---|---|
|  |  |

13-2. In order to reduce the amount of returned merchandise, should a retail business institute a policy of not accepting returns unless the merchandise is defective?

| Reasons for "Yes" | Reasons for "No" |
|---|---|
|  |  |

# PROBLEMS

13-A. One of the problems in operating a retail business is deciding how many brands of an item should be stocked. Before making a decision, it is desirable to know how many different brands and sizes are stocked by competing business firms. Visit a supermarket and a small convenience store and count the number of brands and different package sizes stocked for each of the items listed below. Record your answers in the appropriate spaces on the form.

| Item | Supermarket | | Convenience Store | |
|------|-------------|--|-------------------|--|
| | Number of Brands | Number of Package Sizes | Number of Brands | Number of Package Sizes |
| Sugar | | | | |
| Canned peaches | | | | |
| Frozen pizza | | | | |
| Gelatin dessert | | | | |
| Milk | | | | |

1. Why do you believe there are differences in the number of brands and package sizes carried by the supermarket and the convenience store? _____

   _____

   _____

   _____

2. Why do you believe that more brands and package sizes are available for some products than for others?

   _____

   _____

   _____

   _____

# CONTINUING PROJECT
## Chapter 15 Activities

Business people need a complete set of financial records to make management decisions. This is very important for new businesses, as financial resources are usually limited. In this chapter, you will review the record systems needed for your business and the sources of record-keeping assistance available.

### Data Collection

1. Interview an accountant or review small business management materials. Determine the types of financial records you will need for your business, and the types of record-keeping problems faced by most small businesses.

2. Obtain a copy of a small business financial planning software package for use on a microcomputer. Examine each of the forms and records included with the package and determine the type of information the business would need to acquire to complete each of the forms and records.

### Analysis

1. Develop a detailed set of procedures to be followed in your business for the safe handling of cash. Be certain to consider all situations in which cash will be handled.

2. Prepare a sample three-month cash budget for your business. The budget can be modeled after the example in Chapter 15 of your textbook.

# Study Guide

**Part A**—*Directions:* Indicate your answer to each of the following questions by circling either yes or no in the Answers column.

| | | Answers | | For Scoring |
| :--- | :--- | :---: | :---: | :--- |
| 1. | Are discounts usually allowed on regular charge sales? | yes | no | 1. _____ |
| 2. | Since a customer does not have title to a product purchased on installment, can the product be repossessed if payments are missed? | yes | no | 2. _____ |
| 3. | Have many Americans purchased automobiles on noninstallment credit plans? | yes | no | 3. _____ |
| 4. | Is a major advantage of a business credit card that it takes the place of many separate credit cards? | yes | no | 4. _____ |
| 5. | Are banks NOT permitted to charge for debit card services? | yes | no | 5. _____ |
| 6. | Can a debit card store financial, health, and credit information? | yes | no | 6. _____ |
| 7. | Are the four C's for determining creditworthiness character, capacity, capital, and credit? | yes | no | 7. _____ |
| 8. | When a point system is used for making credit decisions, are the total debts owed by the applicant unimportant? | yes | no | 8. _____ |
| 9. | Is Dun & Bradstreet, Inc. an important source of information on the credit standing of retailers, wholesalers, and manufacturers? | yes | no | 9. _____ |
| 10. | Does the Uniform Commercial Credit Code cover credit conditions related to installment sales contracts? | yes | no | 10. _____ |
| 11. | Can credit be denied a person too old to carry out long-term agreements? | yes | no | 11. _____ |
| 12. | Are single females NOT entitled to the same credit rights as single males? | yes | no | 12. _____ |
| 13. | Does an applicant have the right to know why credit was refused? | yes | no | 13. _____ |
| 14. | Do surveys show that losses from uncollected debts usually amount to about 10 percent of net sales? | yes | no | 14. _____ |
| 15. | Should a small retailer start its own credit department rather than participate in a national credit card service? | yes | no | 15. _____ |
| 16. | If a company uses a cycle billing system, are customers' bills sent out on the last day of the month? | yes | no | 16. _____ |
| 17. | Are the two major objectives of a collection procedure to collect the amount due and to retain the goodwill of the customer? | yes | no | 17. _____ |
| 18. | Is a credit manager likely to skip the final collection step if the amount is small and the customer is financially unable to pay? | yes | no | 18. _____ |
| 19. | Under most state laws, if an account has not been paid within a specified number of years, is collection no longer legally possible? | yes | no | 19. _____ |
| 20. | If an analysis of the accounts receivable record shows that most of the accounts 30 to 60 days old, is it necessary to have some of the customers sign notes? | yes | no | 20. _____ |

**Part B**—*Directions:* For each of the following statements, select the word, or group of words, that best completes the statement. In the Answers column, write the letter corresponding to the answer selected.

| | | Answers | For Scoring |
|---|---|---|---|

1. Which statement is *true* about consumer credit? (a) Consumer credit is extended by the consumer to the retailer. (b) Consumer credit is extended by the retailer to the consumer. (c) Consumer credit is extended by the business to another business. (d) Consumer credit is most commonly used for regular charge purchases. ............  _____ 1. _____

2. An example of consumer credit is a (a) manufacturer giving a retailer thirty days to pay for merchandise, (b) bank providing a business loan, (c) customer purchasing a refrigerator on an installment plan, (d) retailer holding a purchase until the last payment is made. ................  _____ 2. _____

3. Which item is most likely to be purchased under the installment plan? (a) clothing, (b) furniture, (c) small home appliances, (d) groceries. ....................  _____ 3. _____

4. In a regular charge credit plan and in a revolving credit plan, credit passes to the buyer (a) when the first payment is made, (b) at the time of the cycle billing period, (c) at the time of the purchase, (d) when the merchandise is fully paid.  _____ 4. _____

5. Customers who prefer to make one monthly payment even though purchases may be made at many different stores would apply for a (a) business credit card, (b) bank credit card, (c) bank debit card, (d) smart card. ..............................  _____ 5. _____

6. Which statement is *incorrect* about credit in foreign countries? (a) Regular charge cards are commonly used in industrialized countries. (b) Credit card usage continues to grow, especially among the younger generation. (c) The majority of foreign consumers purchase on a cash basis. (d) The older generation uses charge cards more than the younger generation. ........................................  _____ 6. _____

7. What is the best single measure of whether to grant credit to an applicant? (a) Type of job held by the applicant. (b) Length of time applicant has held the job. (c) Total debts owed by the applicant. (d) Past paying record of the applicant.  _____ 7. _____

8. An application for credit usually requests all of the following information *except* (a) years employed, (b) salary expectations, (c) information about the applicant's job, (d) a list of debts. ................  _____ 8. _____

9. Under the Fair Credit Reporting Act, a person (a) has the right to see information in credit agency files but does not have the right to have errors corrected, (b) has the right to see information in credit agency files and also has the right to have errors corrected, (c) does not have a right to have errors corrected in credit agency files, (d) does not have the right to see information in credit agency files. ................  _____ 9. _____

10. If the amount of accounts receivable for a business had steadily increased over the last six months, but its credit sales remained about the same, bad debt losses are likely to (a) increase, (b) decrease, (c) stay about the same, (d) gradually disappear. ................  _____ 10. _____

**Part C**—*Directions:* In the Answers column, write the letter that represents the law listed in Column I that will cover each regulation in Column II.

| Column I (Laws) | Column II (Regulations) | Answers | For Scoring |
|---|---|---|---|
| A. Equal Credit Opportunity Act | 1. Gives women the same credit rights as men. ........... | _____ | 1. _____ |
| B. Truth-in-Lending Act | 2. Requires that a credit applicant who has been refused credit be notified in writing and given a reason...... | _____ | 2. _____ |
| | 3. Requires businesses to reveal the total cost of credit and finance charges on credit forms and statements. | _____ | 3. _____ |
| C. Fair Credit Reporting Act | 4. Gives individuals the right to check personal information appearing in credit agency files.................. | _____ | 4. _____ |
| | 5. Limits losses to $50 to holders of credit cards that have been stolen. ................ | _____ | 5. _____ |

**Directions:** Study each controversial issue carefully. Follow the advice of your teacher before listing in the columns provided reasons why people might answer Yes or No. Your teacher may want you to work with a classmate, talk with others in your community to gather information, or use the library to gather facts.

19-1. With the increasing use of credit and debit cards, will there be nearly a cashless society by the year 2010?

| Reasons for "Yes" | Reasons for "No" |
| --- | --- |
|  |  |

19-2. Consumers have the right to review their credit records under the Fair Credit Reporting Act, even though few do until a problem arises. Consequently, should credit reporting agencies be required to mail to consumers a copy of all information in one's credit file every few years?

| Reasons for "Yes" | Reasons for "No" |
| --- | --- |
|  |  |

# PROBLEMS

**19-A.** On the line provided, record the type of credit plan that should be used in each situation.

1. Customers charge purchases at any time, but must pay the amount owed in full by a specified date, which is usually 30 days. _____

2. Retailers charge merchandise purchased from a wholesaler. _____

3. Customers purchase automobiles and agree to pay an interest charge and make payments for three years.

   _____

4. Customers charge purchases at any time, but have the option of paying a finance charge for making partial payments each month._____

5. Customers make payments, but do not get the item until the last payment is made. _____

   _____

**19-B.** Check whether each situation described below calls for a business credit card, bank credit card, or bank debit card.

| Situation | Business Credit Card | Bank Credit Card | Bank Debit Card |
|---|---|---|---|
| 1. A shopper used one card to buy goods at three different stores. ............. | _____ | _____ | _____ |
| 2. A shopper used a plastic card to buy groceries, but first checked his remaining bank account balance. ...................................................... | _____ | _____ | _____ |
| 3. A retailer withdrew $200 in cash from an automatic teller machine to place in cash registers at the start of the day. ................................. | _____ | _____ | _____ |
| 4. A business person used an affinity card to pay for a client's luncheon. .... | _____ | _____ | _____ |
| 5. A shopper used a department store's credit card to purchase items from advertisements that accompany each month's statement. ........................ | _____ | _____ | _____ |

**19-C.** Prepaid debit cards permit phone companies and other firms to sell plastic phone call cards for fixed amounts such as $6, $9, and $15 to those people who frequently need to make calls from pay phones. For the three types of businesses listed, explain how each might use prepaid debit cards with their customers. The first item is given as an example.

| Type of Business | Purpose of Prepaid Debit Card |
|---|---|
| 0. Telephone company | Use cards to make frequent calls from pay phones. |
| 1. Colleges | _____ |
|  | _____ |
| 2. Banks | _____ |
|  | _____ |
| 3. Bus companies | _____ |
|  | _____ |

**19-D.** Joel Bender has applied for credit to buy a car on the installment plan. He possesses certain characteristics that might affect his request for credit.

1. Classify each characteristic on the form below.

|  |  | Character | Capacity | Capital | Conditions |
|---|---|---|---|---|---|
| a. | Has a steady, high-paying job. ............................. | ___ | ___ | ___ | ___ |
| b. | Does not have much money in cash savings of any kind. .... | ___ | ___ | ___ | ___ |
| c. | Owns a nice home. ........................................ | ___ | ___ | ___ | ___ |
| d. | Poor credit record—rarely pays bills on time. .................. | ___ | ___ | ___ | ___ |
| e. | Frequently loses jobs because of excessive absenteeism. ...... | ___ | ___ | ___ | ___ |
| f. | A recession is affecting his employer's business. ................ | ___ | ___ | ___ | ___ |

2. Is Joel Bender a good candidate for obtaining the credit he desires? _____

   Reasons for your answer: _____

   _____

   _____

**19-E.** The annual sales and the loss on bad debts in each of five business firms are given below. For each firm, determine what percent of the sales is represented by the loss on bad debts.

| Business | Sales | Loss on Bad Debts | Percent |
|---|---|---|---|
| Hart Company | $300,000 | $ 3,000 | _____ |
| Cable & Cable | 200,000 | 1,000 | _____ |
| Bell Corporation | 400,000 | 3,600 | _____ |
| Wahl Appliances | 500,000 | 7,500 | _____ |
| Eastern Corporation | 600,000 | 12,000 | _____ |

**19-F.** On the next page is a credit application form similar to the one shown in Fig. 19-5 on page 465 of your textbook. Use the following information to complete the form. Leave blank any item for which information is not provided.

The applicant is Arnold Prince, 41, who lives at 15 Oak Lane, Houston, TX 77080-5391. His home telephone number is 713-555-6842, and his social security number is 057-28-8373. Mr. Prince is married, has two children, and has owned his own home for five years. His monthly mortgage payment is $850.

The applicant has worked for Cabinets, Inc. (2183 Pine St., Houston, TX) as a carpenter and earns an average of $42,000 a year. The company makes kitchen cabinets that are sold to contractors; the business phone number is 713-555-5921. Prior to obtaining his job five years ago, Mr. Prince worked for the Long Lumber Co. in Houston on Worth Avenue; he was with the company two years.

Arnold Prince's wife, Marilyn, aged 38, is not currently working for an employer. Her social security number is 061-21-7451.

The Princes have their checking and savings accounts at the same bank: First National Bank, Main Street, Houston. The checking account number is 57918 and the money market account number is 57-302. They have a charge account, No. B-78-3564, at Wiley's Department Store with an $89 balance; they buy all their gas for the family car using a Stahl credit card, No. 214-35-892, which they just paid in full. The Princes are requesting $2,500 of credit and would like two credit cards. Sign for Marilyn and Arnold Prince using today's date.

# Kramer's Application for Credit

☐ **Individual Account**—Complete sections A, B, C, E. You may designate one authorized user, for whose payments you will be responsible, by writing only his/her name and relationship in section D.

☐ **Joint Account**—Complete sections A through E.

## Section A—Tell us about yourself

| LAST NAME | FIRST NAME | MIDDLE | | SOCIAL SECURITY NO. | AGE |
|---|---|---|---|---|---|

| HOME ADDRESS | CITY | STATE | ZIP CODE | HOME PHONE ( ) | NO. OF DEPENDENTS |
|---|---|---|---|---|---|

| ☐ OWN   ☐ ROOM & BOARD   ☐ LIVE WITH PARENTS   ☐ RENT FURNISHED ☐ RENT UNFURNISHED   ☐ MOBILE HOME   ☐ OTHER | TIME AT THIS ADDRESS    YRS.    MOS. | MONTHLY RENT/MORTGAGE $ |
|---|---|---|

| PREVIOUS HOME ADDRESS (IF LESS THAN 3 YEARS AT PRESENT ADDRESS) | TIME AT PREVIOUS ADDRESS    YRS.    MOS. |
|---|---|

| NAME AND ADDRESS OF NEAREST RELATIVE NOT LIVING WITH APPLICANT | RELATIVE HOME PHONE ( ) |
|---|---|

## Section B—Tell us about your employment

| BUSINESS OR EMPLOYER | TYPE OF BUSINESS | BUSINESS PHONE ( )    EXT. |
|---|---|---|

| BUSINESS ADDRESS | CITY | STATE | ZIP CODE | EDUCATION   ☐ GRADUATE ☐ COLLEGE ☐ HIGH SCHOOL ☐ ELEMENTARY |
|---|---|---|---|---|

| POSITION OR TITLE | HOW LONG WITH THIS EMPLOYER?    YRS.    MOS. | ANNUAL SALARY $ |
|---|---|---|

| PREVIOUS BUSINESS/EMPLOYER (IF LESS THAN 3 YEARS AT THIS JOB) | HOW LONG?    YRS.    MOS. | POSITION OR TITLE |
|---|---|---|

| OTHER INCOME: ALIMONY, CHILD SUPPORT, OR SEPARATE MAINTENANCE INCOME NEED NOT BE REVEALED IF YOU DO NOT WISH TO HAVE IT CONSIDERED AS A BASIS FOR REPAYING THIS OBLIGATION. | ANNUAL AMOUNT $ | SOURCE |
|---|---|---|

## Section C—Tell us about your credit and banking relationships

| BANK REFERENCES—NAMES OF BANKS AND BRANCH LOCATIONS | ACCOUNT NUMBERS | BALANCE |
|---|---|---|
| 1. | | $ |
| 2. | | $ |

| CREDIT REFERENCES—ACCOUNTS WITH DEPT. STORES, BANK CARDS, OIL COMPANIES | ACCOUNT NUMBERS | BALANCE |
|---|---|---|
| 1. | | $ |
| 2. | | $ |

OUTSTANDING LOANS (NAME OF CREDITOR/CREDIT UNION/FINANCE COMPANY)

| OTHER CREDIT REFERENCES | HAVE YOU EVER HAD ANOTHER KRAMER'S ACCOUNT? | ACCOUNT NO. (IF KNOWN) |
|---|---|---|

## Section D—Information regarding joint applicant or authorized user

| LAST NAME | FIRST NAME | MIDDLE | | SOCIAL SECURITY NO. | AGE |
|---|---|---|---|---|---|

| BUSINESS OR EMPLOYER | TYPE OF BUSINESS | BUSINESS PHONE ( )    EXT. |
|---|---|---|

| BUSINESS ADDRESS | CITY | STATE | ZIP CODE | EDUCATION   ☐ GRADUATE ☐ COLLEGE ☐ HIGH SCHOOL ☐ ELEMENTARY |
|---|---|---|---|---|

| POSITION OR TITLE | HOW LONG WITH THIS EMPLOYER?    YRS.    MOS. | ANNUAL SALARY $ |
|---|---|---|

| RELATIONSHIP TO APPLICANT | OTHER INCOME: ALIMONY, CHILD SUPPORT, OR SEPARATE MAINTENANCE INCOME NEED NOT BE REVEALED IF YOU DO NOT WISH TO HAVE IT CONSIDERED AS A BASIS FOR REPAYING THIS OBLIGATION. | ANNUAL AMOUNT $ | SOURCE |
|---|---|---|---|

## Section E—Optional Accountguard Credit Insurance Plan

Please enroll me in the Accountguard Credit Insurance Plan providing the coverages described and at the cost set forth on the reverse. I understand it is not required to obtain credit and will not be provided unless I sign below and pay the additional cost disclosed on the reverse.

☐ YES _____ , I want ____/____/____ , ☐ NO _____ , I do not want Accountguard Credit Insurance
    initial            birthdate              initial

## Section F—Please sign here and on reverse side

I (We) understand that you may investigate my (our) credit record and may report information concerning the credit experience of the Account for individual and joint accountholders and authorized users to consumer reporting agencies and others.

If Applicant signs on behalf of Joint Applicant, Applicant represents that he or she is authorized to make this application.

I (We) agree to terms of the **RETAIL INSTALLMENT CREDIT AGREEMENT** on reverse side.

**X** _____
APPLICANT'S SIGNATURE                          DATE

**X** _____
JOINT APPLICANT'S SIGNATURE                    DATE

**19-G.** Study the credit card losses in the United States for a recent three-year period for four leading credit card companies: Visa, MasterCard, Discover, and Optima. Then answer the questions.

|  |  |
|---|---|
| Year 1 | $324 million |
| Year 2 | $514 million |
| Year 3 | $720 million |

1. By how much did credit card losses increase from Year 1 to Year 2? _____

2. By how much did credit card losses increase between Year 1 and Year 3? _____

3. Many of the losses occur from credit card crime. If you were a retail store manager, identify two ways that you could protect your store and your customers from credit card losses.

   a. _____

   _____

   b. _____

   _____

**19-H.** Your credit manager handed you the report below. Study it and answer the following questions:

### Comparative Analysis of Past-Due Accounts

| Days Past Due | Current Month | Percent | Prior Month | Percent | Increase or (Decrease) |
|---|---|---|---|---|---|
| 1-30 | $2,580,300 | _____ | $1,335,000 | _____ | $_____ |
| 31-60 | 393,800 | _____ | 171,200 | _____ | _____ |
| 61-90 | 330,700 | _____ | 346,100 | _____ | _____ |
| Over 90 | 94,500 | _____ | 49,500 | _____ | _____ |
|  | $_____ | 100.0% | $_____ | 100.0% | $_____ |

1. Complete the report.

2. By what percent did past-due accounts increase over last month? _____

3. Should the credit manager be concerned? Yes _____ No _____

   Explain: _____

   _____

   _____

4. What are two possible reasons for the changes that have occurred?

a. _____

_____

b. _____

_____

19-I. Indicate by letter the label to be attached to billing statements at each stage in the collection process.

| Days Late in Payment | Billing Stage Label Selected | Label Choices |
|---|---|---|

1. 1-14     _____

2. 15-29     _____

3. 30-44     _____

4. 45-59     _____

5. 60 and over     _____

A.
| Reminder: Your account is now past due. |
|---|

B.
| If we do not receive payment soon, your account will be placed in outside hands. |
|---|

C.
| Your credit is OK, but your payment is long overdue. |
|---|

D.
| We can't pay our bills if we don't get paid. Let us know if something is wrong with your account. |
|---|

E.
| Final Notice! Unless payment is received at once, your account will be turned over to a collection agency. |
|---|

# CONTINUING PROJECT
## Chapter 19 Activities

The nature of your new business means that you will not be extending credit to customers. However, you will likely have the opportunity to receive trade credit from your suppliers. In these activities, you will develop policies to determine when to accept trade credit.

### Data Collection

1. For a potential supplier of products to your business, determine policies for extending trade credit and the credit terms offered.

2. Contact a credit card company and determine the procedures a business must follow to accept that credit card from customers and process the credit transactions for payment. Determine the costs of that credit card to the business.

### Analysis

1. Assume that you have purchased $1,200 of products from a wholesaler. The wholesaler will extend credit for 30 days or will give a cash discount for payment within 10 days. What is meant by the terms 2/10, n/30? Does it pay to take discounts? What discount must the supplier offer in order for you to consider borrowing money from a bank at 10% interest for 20 days to pay the debt within 10 days?

2. Develop several policy statements to guide you in determining when to use trade credit and the amount of trade credit to use.

# Study Guide

**Part A**—*Directions:* Indicate your answer to each of the following questions by circling either yes or no in the Answers column.

|  |  | Answers | For Scoring |
|---|---|---|---|
| 1. | Is it true that most businesses will never be faced with losses that are so great the business could fail? | yes no | 1. _____ |
| 2. | Can businesses make plans so they can continue to operate even when faced with costly losses? | yes no | 2. _____ |
| 3. | Can businesses usually predict whether specific losses will occur and the amounts of those losses? | yes no | 3. _____ |
| 4. | Do insurance companies provide insurance for those losses that are difficult to predict? | yes no | 4. _____ |
| 5. | Do insurance rates vary based on the type of risks and the history of loss for the type of risk? | yes no | 5. _____ |
| 6. | Is it illegal for insurance companies to cancel property or liability insurance contracts? | yes no | 6. _____ |
| 7. | May you purchase property insurance even if you do not have an insurable interest in the property? | yes no | 7. _____ |
| 8. | With a deductible, is the insured responsible for part of the loss in return for a lower premium? | yes no | 8. _____ |
| 9. | Does coinsurance divide a loss on a percentage basis between the insurer and the insured? | yes no | 9. _____ |
| 10. | Is reinsurance used when the insured finds a second company to insure a property after the original policy has been canceled? | yes no | 10. _____ |
| 11. | Do many insurance agents sell insurance for several insurance companies? | yes no | 11. _____ |
| 12. | Since all insurance agents offer the same services and prices for insurance, is it acceptable to purchase insurance from any agent? | yes no | 12. _____ |
| 13. | Is it possible that a fire insurance policy may not cover the equipment and supplies in the building in the event of a fire? | yes no | 13. _____ |
| 14. | Should companies purchase more fire insurance than the actual cost of the property being insured in order to make money if a loss occurs? | yes no | 14. _____ |
| 15. | Are businesses are able to purchase insurance that will compensate for loss of income if the business cannot operate due to a fire or storm damage? | yes no | 15. _____ |
| 16. | Is a transportation company responsible for any loss that occurs while products are being shipped so the owner of the goods will not need insurance? | yes no | 16. _____ |
| 17. | If comprehensive insurance is purchased on a vehicle, will it cover all losses in the event of an accident? | yes no | 17. _____ |
| 18. | Do Health Maintenance Organizations (HMOs) offer an alternative to traditional health insurance? | yes no | 18. _____ |
| 19. | Are the person or persons receiving payment of life insurance known as beneficiaries? | yes no | 19. _____ |
| 20. | Is insurance that covers businesses for losses that result from the operation of the business known as liability insurance? | yes no | 20. _____ |

**Part B**—*Directions:* For each of the following statements, select the word, or group of words, that best completes the statement. In the Answers column, write the letter corresponding to the answer selected.

|  |  | Answers | For Scoring |
|--|--|--|--|

1. Which of the following types of losses would NOT usually be insured by a business? (a) fire, (b) death of the owner, (c) storm damage to vehicles, (d) shoplifting losses. ............................................................  _____  1. _____

2. Of the following people, who has an insurable interest in the business? (a) a customer of the business, (b) the owner of the property next to the business, (c) the banker who provided a loan to the business, (d) the insurance agent. .......  _____  2. _____

3. If an insurance policy carries a deductible, the insured will (a) pay a lower premium, (b) pay a higher premium, (c) receive a higher settlement in case of a loss, (d) deduct the amount of any loss from the premium owed. ...................  _____  3. _____

4. When a property insurance policy contains a coinsurance clause and the property is insured for the required value, the insured will pay the coinsurance amount for (a) a partial loss, (b) any loss, (c) a loss that exceeds the amount of the premium, (d) a total loss. ................................................................  _____  4. _____

5. Which of the following is NOT a primary objective in buying insurance? (a) Get the proper coverage of risks. (b) Make sure claims will be paid if a loss occurs. (c) Purchase the least amount of insurance possible. (d) All of the responses. .............................................................................................  _____  5. _____

6. Which of the following would be an example of extended coverage on a fire insurance policy? (a) life insurance, (b) flood insurance, (c) health insurance, (d) vehicle insurance. ...............................................................................  _____  6. _____

7. Which of the following procedures should businesses consider using to protect important documents and records? (a) Make duplicate copies of all records. (b) Store copies in a separate location from originals. (c) Prepare and practice a disaster plan. (d) All of the responses. .......................................................  _____  7. _____

8. Insurance that provides protection against damage caused by the insured's vehicle to other people or property is known as (a) liability insurance, (b) comprehensive insurance, (c) collision insurance, (d) medical payments insurance. ....  _____  8. _____

9. Which of the following is NOT insurance that is related to the employees of a business? (a) health, (b) liability, (c) no-fault, (d) life. ...................................  _____  9. _____

10. If a business has purchased title insurance on a piece of property and it is later learned that there is a problem with the title, the insured will (a) be able to keep the property, (b) receive payment for losses resulting from giving up the property, (c) have to pay for any loss, (d) receive a refund of the amount of the premium. .............................................................................................  _____  10. _____

**Part C**—*Directions:* In the Answers column, write the letter of the word or expression in Column I that most closely matches each statement in Column II.

| Column I | Column II | Answers | For Scoring |
|--|--|--|--|
| A. Insurer | 1. The person or organization covered by the insurance policy. ............................................ | _____ | 1. _____ |
| B. Policyholder | 2. The uncertainty that a loss may occur. .......... | _____ | 2. _____ |
| C. Insured | 3. The person or business purchasing insurance. | _____ | 3. _____ |
| D. Peril | 4. A company that sells insurance. .................... | _____ | 4. _____ |
| E. Risk | 5. The cause of a loss for a person or organization. | _____ | 5. _____ |

**Directions:** Study each controversial issue carefully. Follow the advice of your teacher before listing in the columns provided reasons why people might answer Yes or No. Your teacher may want you to work with a classmate, talk with others in your community, or use the library to gather facts.

20-1. Should companies rely on product liability insurance to cover possible losses resulting from customers who are injured by the companies' products rather than spending a great deal of money to develop safer products?

| Reasons for "Yes" | Reasons for "No" |
| --- | --- |
|  |  |

20-2. Should businesses be responsible for providing health insurance for all full-time and part-time employees even if it reduces or eliminates the amount of profit the businesses can make?

| Reasons for "Yes" | Reasons for "No" |
| --- | --- |
|  |  |

# PROBLEMS

**20-A.** The Keystone Fire Insurance Company has issued policies on different buildings with varying amounts and coinsurance clauses as listed below. Also listed are the various amounts of loss caused by fire. For each policy, calculate the amount of the loss to be paid by the insurance company.

| Policy No. | Value of Property | Amount of Insurance | Coinsurance Clause | Fire Loss | Amount to Be Paid by Insurance Company |
|---|---|---|---|---|---|
| A-165592 | $75,000 | $50,000 | 80% | $38,000 | $ |
| A-191477 | $100,000 | $80,000 | 80% | $22,000 | $ |
| A-244310 | $200,000 | $180,000 | 90% | $200,000 | $ |
| A-295555 | $90,000 | $70,000 | 100% | $18,000 | $ |
| A-312616 | $20,000 | $15,000 | none | $16,000 | $ |

**20-B.** The Autocity Taxi Company owns and operates a fleet of 100 taxis. It pays an annual insurance premium of $480 per taxi. One-third of the premium pays for liability and medical payments coverage while two-thirds provides collision and comprehensive coverage. During the past five years, Autocity has had the following record of losses covered by collision and comprehensive insurance:

> Year 1 $40,000
> Year 2 $28,000
> Year 3 $23,000
> Year 4 $36,000
> Year 5 $38,000

Autocity is considering dropping its coverage for collision and comprehensive and putting the money it saves into an account to pay for damage to its taxis.

1. If Autocity had followed its plan for the past five years, how much money could have been saved?

_____

2. What other factors should Autocity consider before deciding to drop the insurance coverage?

_____

**20-C.** The Monumental Insurance Company sells life insurance. Premiums for each $1,000 of ordinary life insurance are shown on the next page. The smallest policy the company sells is for $5,000 coverage, but premiums may be paid once a year (annually), twice a year (semiannually), or four times a year (quarterly). Study the table and answer the following questions:

1. What is the quarterly premium for Beth Williams? She purchased a $50,000 policy at age 34.

_____

2. What is the semiannual premium for John VanDyke? He purchased a $20,000 policy at age 25.

_____

| Age Nearest Birthday | Premiums | | |
|---|---|---|---|
| | Annually | Semiannually | Quarterly |
| 25 | $10.13 | $5.27 | $2.74 |
| 26 | $10.50 | $5.46 | $2.84 |
| 27 | $10.86 | $5.65 | $2.93 |
| 28 | $11.26 | $5.86 | $3.04 |
| 29 | $11.68 | $6.07 | $3.15 |
| 30 | $12.07 | $6.28 | $3.26 |
| 31 | $12.47 | $6.48 | $3.37 |
| 32 | $12.90 | $6.71 | $3.48 |
| 33 | $13.34 | $6.94 | $3.60 |
| 34 | $13.81 | $7.18 | $3.73 |
| 35 | $14.30 | $7.44 | $3.86 |

3. What is the annual premium for Earl McCauley? He purchased a $35,000 policy at age 28.

   _____

4. What is the yearly premium for Alice Evans, who purchased a $15,000 policy at age 30, but pays premiums quarterly? _____

5. If Alice Evans paid premiums annually rather than quarterly, how much would she save yearly?

   _____

6. Give a reason why total premiums are less if paid once a year than premiums paid four times a year.

   _____

**20-D.** For each type of loss suffered by a business listed in the center column of the chart below, select the type of business insurance from the column on the left that would protect against that loss. Write the correct answer in the column on the right.

| Business Insurance | Loss Suffered | Answers |
|---|---|---|
| A. Business-Income insurance | 1. A customer's business went bankrupt after purchasing an expensive piece of equipment. | 1. _____ |
| B. Transportation insurance | 2. An adjoining landowner disputes the property boundary of the business. | 2. _____ |
| C. Burglary, robbery, and theft insurance | 3. A company's delivery van is stolen after it has been loaded with merchandise. | 3. _____ |
| D. Credit insurance | 4. After an unusually heavy rainstorm that flooded a factory, the business was unable to resume production for two weeks. | 4. _____ |
| E. Property insurance | 5. A business cashes a payroll check and later learns that blank checks had been stolen, filled in, and then cashed. | 5. _____ |
| F. Title insurance | 6. After sending a shipment to a new customer in another country, the business learns the customer's bank has failed, so payment cannot be made. | 6. _____ |
| G. Export-Credit insurance | 7. An oil-importing company lost part of a shipment when the ship carrying crude oil was damaged in a collision. | 7. _____ |

**20-E.** A company offers its employees a choice of enrolling in a traditional health insurance program or in a Health Maintenance Organization (HMO). The monthly cost of the traditional program is $85 for each employee. Employees must then pay a 20% deductible charge on all routine medical services until they have paid $500 in a year. For major medical expenses, the employees are responsible for 10% of the costs up to a maximum of $1,500 a year. Employees participating in the HMO pay a monthly cost of $140 a month for individual coverage. For that premium, all medical costs are covered and the employee participates in all HMO services. Compare the advantages and disadvantages of the two health insurance plans for employees.

| Traditional Health Insurance | |
|---|---|
| Advantages | Disadvantages |
| | |

| Health Maintenance Organization | |
|---|---|
| Advantages | Disadvantages |
| | |

**20-F.** Identify the following risks as normally being insurable or noninsurable by placing a check mark in the appropriate column.

|  | Insurable | Noninsurable |
|---|---|---|
| 1. Due to a cold and rainy summer season, a clothing store, unable to sell much of its inventory of swimwear, cannot pay the supplier. .............. | _____ | _____ |
| 2. Because of improper storage procedures, a manufacturer finds that a large quantity of the raw materials used in production has been damaged and cannot be used. ............................................................ | _____ | _____ |
| 3. A trucking company has had a very large contract with a wholesaler for the past five years. During the last six months, several of the older trucks have had an unusual number of breakdowns resulting in problems delivering the wholesaler's orders. As a result, the wholesaler has refused to sign a new contract with the trucking company. ................ | _____ | _____ |
| 4. An insurance company has computer records of all policies and stores them in a vault in another city to protect against loss in case of fire or other damage to its headquarters building. However, the company would still face a significant expense if the original records were destroyed. ................................................................. | _____ | _____ |
| 5. A company had just purchased several new vehicles that were parked on the street waiting to be serviced before they were picked up by the company's salespeople. During the night, an uninsured driver lost control of his car while driving by the vehicles. Three of the vehicles had major damage while two others had minor damage. ......................... | _____ | _____ |

**20-G.** Calculate the annual premium costs for the following insurance policies:

1. Fire insurance on a $360,000 building at a rate of $1.80 per $1,000 of value. $ _____

2. Liability insurance on a truck valued at $23,400 at a rate of $.63 per $100 of value. $ _____

3. Disability insurance on an annual salary of $32,500 at a rate of .5 percent of the annual salary.

   $ _____

4. Credit life insurance on the purchase of a $14,000 automobile for which the purchaser finances 80 percent of the cost. The insurance rate is $.50 per $100. $ _____

5. Insurance against shoplifting on an average inventory value of $1,590,000. The insurance rate is $2.20 per $1,000 of average inventory. $ _____

# CONTINUING PROJECT
## Chapter 20 Activities

While insurance is often expensive, new businesses must be protected from possible losses that would cause the business to fail. This chapter assists you in determining the types and costs of insurance you will need.

### Data Collection

1. Interview an insurance agent to determine the types of insurance coverage available for small businesses, the protection provided, and the cost of each type of insurance.
2. Review newspapers for several days and identify the types of risks and losses suffered by businesses that were reported. Identify which appeared to be insured and which were not.

### Analysis

1. Prepare a list of the types of insurance you will need and the amount of coverage needed for each. Also list any insurable risks you have decided not to protect with insurance and a justification for each decision.
2. Identify all noninsurable risks that could affect your business. Suggest methods of avoiding or reducing each of the risks identified.

# Study Guide

**Part A**—*Directions:* Indicate your answer to each of the following questions by circling either yes or no in the Answers column.

| | | Answers | | For Scoring |
|---|---|---|---|---|
| 1. | Of all the resources used by a business, are people the most important to the success of the business? ................................................ | yes no | | 1. _____ |
| 2. | Are human resources managers the only managers that work with people? .... | yes no | | 2. _____ |
| 3. | Is ensuring the health and safety of employees a major activity of the human resources department? ................................................ | yes no | | 3. _____ |
| 4. | Are human resources activities unnecessary in small companies? ................ | yes no | | 4. _____ |
| 5. | Does the productivity of employees compared to the expenses of wages and benefits determine whether a company will be profitable or not? ................ | yes no | | 5. _____ |
| 6. | Are the training responsibilities of human resources completed once orientation training has been provided to new employees? ................................ | yes no | | 6. _____ |
| 7. | Is it illegal today to search for the most qualified applicants when attempting to hire new employees? ................................................ | yes no | | 7. _____ |
| 8. | Is the first step in hiring a new employee establishing the need for a new hire? | yes no | | 8. _____ |
| 9. | Is the job specification a form sent to the human resources department requesting that a position be filled? ................................................ | yes no | | 9. _____ |
| 10. | Is it illegal to fill a vacancy with a current employee from another job in the company? ................................................ | yes no | | 10. _____ |
| 11. | Are employment agencies businesses that actively recruit, evaluate, and help people prepare for and locate jobs? ................................ | yes no | | 11. _____ |
| 12. | Is a telephone call the most effective way to gather information about a job applicant from those people listed as references? ................................ | yes no | | 12. _____ |
| 13. | Do some companies involve experienced employees from the department in which the applicant will work in the actual interview of applicants? ............ | yes no | | 13. _____ |
| 14. | Is it illegal to require applicants to pass a physical exam before they are hired to work for a company? ................................................ | yes no | | 14. _____ |
| 15. | Should every employee have an equal opportunity to receive promotions for which they are qualified? ................................................ | yes no | | 15. _____ |
| 16. | Is a layoff the release of an employee from the company due to inappropriate work behavior? ................................................ | yes no | | 16. _____ |
| 17. | Is it important to provide an exit interview whenever an employee leaves a company? ................................................ | yes no | | 17. _____ |
| 18. | Do wages describe compensation paid on an hourly basis while salary describes compensation paid on other than an hourly basis? ................................ | yes no | | 18. _____ |
| 19. | Have some companies divided one job between two part-time employees through a program called job sharing? ................................................ | yes no | | 19. _____ |
| 20. | Did the Social Security Act establish a minimum wage that must be paid to employees by those businesses included in the law? ................................ | yes no | | 20. _____ |

**Part B**—*Directions:* For each of the following statements, select the word, or group of words, that best completes the statement. In the Answers column, write the letter corresponding to the answer selected.

| | Answers | For Scoring |
|---|---|---|

1. A very formal set of relationships exists between management and employees if the company has a(n) (a) high wage rate, (b) employee assistance program, (c) labor union, (d) human resources department. ........................ _____ 1. _____

2. The first step in processing applicants for a job is (a) an applicant interview, (b) reviewing applications to eliminate unqualified applicants, (c) checking an applicant's references, (d) administering knowledge and skill tests. ............... _____ 2. _____

3. Generally, the decision about whether a person should apply and be considered for promotion is made by (a) the immediate supervisor and the employee, (b) the employee and his/her family, (c) an employment agency, (d) an employee's co-workers. ........................ _____ 3. _____

4. The extent to which people enter and leave employment in a business during a year is known as (a) layoffs, (b) the application process, (c) transfers and terminations, (d) employment turnover. ........................ _____ 4. _____

5. The money and other benefits people receive for work is called (a) wages, (b) salary, (c) compensation, (d) employee assistance. ........................ _____ 5. _____

6. The process of ranking jobs according to their value based on specific characteristics of each job is (a) performance evaluation, (b) job evaluation, (c) employee evaluation, (d) an illegal business practice. ........................ _____ 6. _____

7. If Jacob received a $500 increase in salary last year and inflation increased his cost of living by $300, Jacob's real wages will have (a) increased, (b) decreased, (c) not been affected, (d) none of the responses. ........................ _____ 7. _____

8. Regular payments made to employees after their retirement are (a) profit sharing, (b) cafeteria payments, (c) bonuses, (d) pensions. ........................ _____ 8. _____

9. The Department of Labor enforces safety and health standards in businesses as a result of the (a) Fair Labor Standards Act, (b) Occupational Safety and Health Act, (c) Social Security Act, (d) Workers' Compensation Act. ........................ _____ 9. _____

10. In order to qualify for employment under the Americans with Disabilities Act, disabled individuals must be able to (a) get to work, (b) pass a test of complex job requirements, (c) perform the basic functions of the job, (d) prove they have been discriminated against. ........................ _____ 10. _____

**Part C**—*Directions:* In the Answers column, write the letter of the word or expression in Column I that most closely matches each statement in Column II.

| Column I | Column II | Answers | For Scoring |
|---|---|---|---|
| A. Promotion | 1. Compensation of employees based on the number of units of production. ........................ | _____ | 1. _____ |
| B. Seniority | 2. The advancement of an employee within a company to a position with more authority and responsibility. ........................ | _____ | 2. _____ |
| C. Transfer | 3. Payment for performance that exceeds a standard. ........................ | _____ | 3. _____ |
| D. Piece-rate | 4. The length of time an employee is with a company. ........................ | _____ | 4. _____ |
| E. Bonus | 5. The assignment of an employee to another job in the company which involves the same types of responsibilities and authority. ........................ | _____ | 5. _____ |

**Directions:** Study each controversial issue carefully. Follow the advice of your teacher before listing in the columns provided reasons why people might answer Yes or No. Your teacher may want you to work with a classmate, talk with others in your community to gather information, or use the library to gather facts.

21-1. If there is a major conflict between the needs of a company and the needs of employees, should personnel in the human resources department take the side of the business?

| Reasons for "Yes" | Reasons for "No" |
| --- | --- |
|  |  |

21-2. Do laws such as the Occupational Safety and Health Act and the Americans with Disabilities Act provide examples of too much government interference in the operations of businesses?

| Reasons for "Yes" | Reasons for "No" |
| --- | --- |
|  |  |

# PROBLEMS

**21-A.** The following items describe steps to be taken in hiring employees. Number the steps to show the correct order for completing the employment procedures. The first step should be the first activity completed, the second step should be the second activity, and so forth.

| | | |
|---|---|---|
| _____ | A. | Conduct a general interview with applicant. |
| _____ | B. | Prepare a job specification card. |
| _____ | C. | Hire the most qualified applicant. |
| _____ | D. | Provide detailed information about the job and introduce to fellow workers. |
| _____ | E. | Have applicant fill out an application blank. |
| _____ | F. | Check references, education, and past work experiences of the applicant. |
| _____ | G. | Provide a follow-up on the new employee. |
| _____ | H. | Submit an employment requisition. |
| _____ | I. | Have department head interview applicant. |
| _____ | J. | Recruit qualified applicants. |

**21-B.** The human resources manager asks you to prepare a report on the labor turnover in the manufacturing industry over the last eight years. Use the data and the firm below to figure out the percentage of labor turnover.

| Year No. | Avergage Number of Employees During the Year | Number of Employees Who Terminated Their Employment During the Year | Percentage of Labor Turnover |
|---|---|---|---|
| 1 | 3,125 | 100 | % |
| 2 | 3,150 | 156 | % |
| 3 | 3,200 | 162 | % |
| 4 | 3,050 | 150 | % |
| 5 | 3,400 | 170 | % |
| 6 | 3,750 | 210 | % |
| 7 | 3,300 | 230 | % |
| 8 | 3,250 | 270 | % |

**21-C.** Obtain the classified section of a newspaper and clip an example of an employment advertisement that contains appropriate information for potential applicants. Next, clip an example of an ad that does not contain appropriate information. Attach both ads to this page in the space provided below. Below the ads, write why you believe the ads are good or poor.

| Good employment ad | Poor employment ad |
|---|---|
| | |

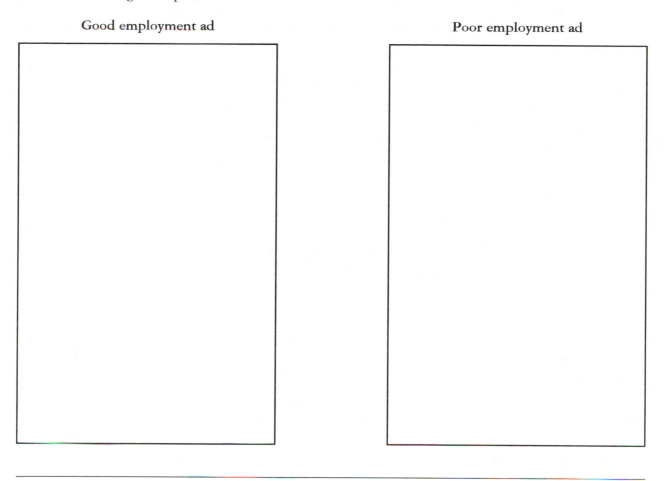

**21-D.** The Storeze Company employs six salespeople to sell its products. Last year each salesperson sold the following amounts:

| Salesperson | Amount of Sales | Straight Salary | Commission | Salary and Bonus |
|---|---|---|---|---|
| Jackson | $569,000 | | | |
| Klein | $630,000 | | | |
| Drase | $520,500 | | | |
| Teng | $605,200 | | | |
| Russo | $723,000 | | | |
| Astor | $502,600 | | | |
| Total Salary Costs | | | | |

The company is considering several compensation plans. Salespeople are currently paid a straight salary of $27,000 a year. Proposed compensation plans are (1) a straight commission of 4.5 percent on all sales, and (2) a salary of $20,000 plus a bonus of 9 percent on all sales above $500,000.

1. Complete the table on the previous page to show the salary of each salesperson for the three compensation plans. Also compute the cost of each plan for the company.

2. Write a recommendation for the company in which you justify one of the plans based on this chart's information._____

_____

_____

_____

_____

_____

_____

_____

_____

21-E. The Broaddex Company uses a job evaluation system to establish the rate of pay for each job. Using a point system, the company evaluates each job and then pays $25 for each point. Evaluations for three jobs are listed in the chart below. Determine the total points and rate of pay for each job.

| | | Factors Evaluated | Job #1 | Job #2 | Job #3 |
|---|---|---|---|---|---|
| Skill | | | | | |
| | 1. | Training needed | 30 | 60 | 45 |
| | 2. | Experience required | 50 | 80 | 70 |
| | 3. | Versatility | 80 | 30 | 60 |
| | 4. | Human relations | 20 | 90 | 50 |
| Responsibility | | | | | |
| | 5. | For details | 75 | 80 | 65 |
| | 6. | For quality | 30 | 80 | 90 |
| | 7. | For other people | 0 | 80 | 20 |
| Effort | | | | | |
| | 8. | Physical | 95 | 30 | 45 |
| | 9. | Mental | 70 | 90 | 60 |
| Conditions | | | | | |
| | 10. | Working environment | 50 | 30 | 70 |
| | 11. | Exposure to danger | 50 | 35 | 10 |

_____

Total Points

_____

Rate of Pay

_____

21-F. If you are currently employed, use your job duties to complete the following Job Specification Form. If you are not employed, interview a family member or friend who has a job and use that information to complete the form.

## Job Specification Form

Company: _____ Department: _____

Job Title: _____ Rate of Pay: From _____ to _____

Previous Job in Organization Chart: _____

Next Job in Organization Chart: _____

Supervisor's Job Title: _____

### QUALIFICATIONS

Education:

Experience:

Physical Requirements:

Specific Skills or Abilities Required:

Training Provided:

### JOB REQUIREMENTS

Major Job Tasks:

Specific Job Duties:

Number of Work Hours Required per Week:
     Maximum_____    Minimum_____

Normal Work Schedule:
     Daily:

     Weekly:

Employee Benefits Provided:
     Vacation:

     Insurance:

     Other:

21-G. Complete the following chart illustrating the costs of fringe benefits for six companies.

| Company | Total Payroll | Fringe Benefit % of Total Payroll | Fringe Benefit Costs | Total Payroll and Benefits |
|---------|---------------|-----------------------------------|----------------------|----------------------------|
| A | $960,500 | 32.00% | | |
| B | | 28.50% | | $1,350,000 |
| C | $495,000 | | $170,775 | |
| D | | 30.00% | $ 36,500 | |
| E | $827,600 | | | $ 910,000 |
| F | | 25.00% | | $1,500,000 |

178

# CONTINUING PROJECT
## Chapter 21 Activities

A small business often has only a few employees. Each employee is very important to the success of the business. When you begin to hire employees for your business, you will need procedures designed to obtain excellent employees.

### Data Collection

1. Review the employment ads in your newspaper for several days. Identify ads for employment in fast food businesses. Study the qualifications and descriptions of duties listed.
2. Interview the manager of a fast food restaurant. Discuss the problems in finding and hiring qualified employees. Review how compensation decisions are made.

### Analysis

1. Develop a job specification for an employee you would hire for your business. Then write the copy for a newspaper advertisement you would use to recruit potential employees.
2. Develop a specific set of procedures to follow in hiring and providing orientation for new employees.
3. Identify the advantages and disadvantages of two compensation plans you would consider using for employees.

# Study Guide

**Part A**—*Directions:* Indicate your answer to each of the following questions by circling either yes or no in the Answers column.

|  |  | Answers | For Scoring |
|---|---|---|---|

1. Is it likely that employees who look very promising when they are hired may have problems because they cannot perform their jobs adequately? ............... yes no 1. _____

2. Do most businesses find that training programs are not able to pay for themselves through improved employee performance? ........................................ yes no 2. _____

3. Is it unusual for employees to be promoted into a supervisory position without adequate training for the new job? ........................................ yes no 3. _____

4. Do U.S. businesses spend over 40 billion dollars each year on formal training programs for their employees? ........................................ yes no 4. _____

5. Does regular, effective training result in employees who are more satisfied with their jobs? ........................................ yes no 5. _____

6. Do companies on average spend about 10 percent of their payrolls each year on training? ........................................ yes no 6. _____

7. Is one of the primary methods of formal training having an employee use manuals and written materials to learn a new procedure? ........................................ yes no 7. _____

8. Is the training in businesses very similar to the way classes are taught in school? yes no 8. _____

9. Is training done in a classroom usually short-term, often one or two days in length? ........................................ yes no 9. _____

10. Is one of the disadvantages of classroom training that it is not very flexible? .. yes no 10. _____

11. When salespeople learn telemarketing skills in a room set up like the work environment with computers and telephones, are they participating in laboratory training? ........................................ yes no 11. _____

12. Is laboratory training usually less expensive than classroom training? ............ yes no 12. _____

13. Is the most frequently used type of training in business on-the-job training? . yes no 13. _____

14. Is apprenticeship training organized and managed by labor unions and management? ........................................ yes no 14. _____

15. In order to reduce stress, should orientation programs avoid telling new employees about company rules, policies, and procedures? ................... yes no 15. _____

16. Is it best to move quickly through an orientation program in order to get new employees on to the job as soon as possible? ............................. yes no 16. _____

17. Is effective training provided in short blocks rather than one long training session? ........................................ yes no 17. _____

18. Is it appropriate to involve employee groups in identifying training needs for a company? ........................................ yes no 18. _____

19. Should businesses avoid evaluating their training programs so employees will not have to worry about the quality of their performance? ...................... yes no 19. _____

20. Should employees be formally evaluated by their supervisors or managers at least once or twice a year? ........................................ yes no 20. _____

**Part B**—*Directions:* For each of the following statements, select the word, or group of words, that best completes the statement. In the Answers column, write the letter corresponding to the answer selected.

| | Answers | For Scoring |
|---|---|---|

1. Which of the following would be a cost to businesses that do not have effective training programs? (a) Employee turnover will increase. (b) Supplies and materials will be wasted. (c) Employees or customers can be injured. (d) All are costs of ineffective training. ............................................................................. _____ 1._____

2. The estimated annual total cost of formal and informal training to business in the United States is (a) just under $100 million, (b) about $10 billion, (c) about $200 billion, (d) over $1 trillion. .............................................................. _____ 2._____

3. International business has forced U.S. businesses to emphasize employee training because (a) it is required by the U.S. government, (b) U.S. employees must be more productive to justify higher wages, (c) U.S. products are not of high quality, (d) all of the responses. ................................................................ _____ 3._____

4. Using the average percentage of payroll costs U.S. companies spend on training, if a company has a payroll of $100 million, the amount spent on training will be (a) $100,000, (b) $1 million, (c) $10 million, (d) $100 million. ......... _____ 4._____

5. Of the following choices, the one that will likely be the most expensive is (a) laboratory training, (b) classroom training, (c) orientation training, (d) informal training. ............................................................................................ _____ 5._____

6. The oldest form of formal training is (a) laboratory training, (b) apprentice training, (c) classroom training, (d) management training. ............................ _____ 6._____

7. Which of the following is NOT an effective practice in new employee training? (a) Use the language of the business even if employees do not yet know it. (b) Provide materials for employees to study. (c) Ask employees plenty of questions to check understanding. (d) Explain the importance of the things employees see during the orientation. ................................................................................. _____ 7._____

8. The first step in developing a training program is to (a) develop written objectives, (b) identify the content of the program, (c) develop formal evaluation methods, (d) identify training needs. ..................................................................... _____ 8._____

9. Which of the following would be the most effective evaluation method? (a) Each employee is rated on a scale of 1-5. (b) Each evaluator determines his or her own criteria to be used. (c) A list of specific job skills is developed in the form of a checklist. (d) None of the methods listed would be effective. .......... _____ 9._____

10. Which of the following is NOT a step that should be followed in achieving a successful evaluation conference? (a) Tell the employee whether the conference is formal or informal. (b) Schedule the conference for a short time at the employee's workstation. (c) Discuss both strengths and weak areas of employee performance. (d) End the conference by offering encouragement. ....................................... _____ 10._____

**Part C**—*Directions:* Read each of the following statements carefully. For each characteristic of an effective training program, write an E in the Answers column. For each ineffective characteristic, write an I in the Answers column.

| | Answers | For Scoring |
|---|---|---|

1. Is related to knowledge the trainee already has developed. ............................ _____ 1._____

2. Shows how things are done but avoids the reasons so the trainee isn't confused. _____ 2._____

3. Encourages the trainee to be as accurate as possible from the very beginning. _____ 3._____

4. Teaches the simple procedures first before progressing to the more difficult ones. ............................................................................................................. _____ 4._____

5. Is done in short time blocks with a variety of activities. ................................. _____ 5._____

**Directions:** Study each controversial issue carefully. Follow the advice of your teacher before listing in the columns provided reasons why people might answer Yes or No. Your teacher may want you to work with a classmate, talk with others in your community to gather information, or use the library to gather facts.

22-1. If businesses have access to a large supply of well-qualified prospective employees, should they terminate current employees whose skills become out-of-date rather than investing the time and money needed to retrain them and hire new, qualified employees?

| Reasons for "Yes" | Reasons for "No" |
|---|---|
|  |  |

22-2. Do employees who are experts in their jobs with many years of experience make the best trainers when compared to employees with less skill and experience but who have a background in education and training?

| Reasons for "Yes" | Reasons for "No" |
|---|---|
|  |  |

# PROBLEMS

**22-A.** The manager of the training department of the Zidran Company studied the amount of training provided during the month of April. The following data show the hours of training provided for the employee groups:

| | |
|---|---|
| New employee training | 68 hours |
| Secretarial/Clerical personnel | 26 hours |
| Sales training | 55 tours |
| Production personnel | 42 hours |
| Supervisor training | 18 hours |
| Executive development | 22 hours |

1. What was the total number of training hours provided during April?   _____ hours

2. Calculate the percentage of total hours provided to each of the employee groups listed:

New employees            _____%

Secretarial/Clerical        _____%

Sales                    _____%

Production                _____%

Supervisors              _____%

Executives               _____%

3. Construct a pie chart comparing the training hours provided to the employee groups.

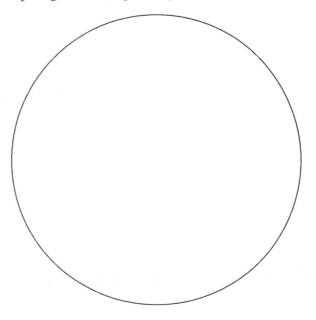

**22-B.** For each of the situations given on the next page, identify which of the following would be the most appropriate type of training by writing the letter of the type of training in the blank space.

    A.     Classroom training
    B.     Laboratory training
    C.     On-the-job training
    D.     Apprenticeship training

_____ 1. An experienced salesperson is assigned a new territory and will be supervised by a different sales manager.

_____ 2. The company's supervisors need to become familiar with a new evaluation procedure that has been developed by the human resource department.

_____ 3. A new plant is opening in a community in one year and a serious housing shortage is expected due to new employees moving into the community. The carpenters' union is working with construction companies in the area to train new carpenters.

_____ 4. Assembly of components for a computer are done in a dust-free enclosure where specialists manipulate robots to fasten circuits to a circuit board. The procedure requires 100 percent accuracy so new assembly personnel must be well-trained.

_____ 5. A retailer has received a number of complaints about being treated indifferently by salespeople. The retailer decides to provide training for all employees on effective human-relations skills.

22-C. Study the following descriptions of training situations. Determine if the description indicates an effective or ineffective training procedure. Place a check mark in the appropriate column.

| Training Situation | Effective | Ineffective |
|---|---|---|
| 1. After an employee has been shown a new procedure, the employee must practice the procedure continually until it can be performed correctly. | _____ | _____ |
| 2. After a trainer demonstrates a new procedure to employees, the trainer asks the employees to identify things they have done similar to the procedure they are learning. | _____ | _____ |
| 3. When employees are introduced to a new job, the trainer tells them they will learn it better if they concentrate on the most difficult parts first and save the easier parts until later. | _____ | _____ |
| 4. A trainer believes that employees will be more motivated to learn if they are criticized the first several times they make mistakes. | _____ | _____ |
| 5. When employees are learning a new skill, the first concern is that they can perform it accurately. | _____ | _____ |
| 6. If employees spend a great deal of time practicing a new skill, they will become bored; therefore, the trainer gives them very little time to practice. | _____ | _____ |
| 7. A variety of activities are used to help an employee learn a procedure rather than only one activity. | _____ | _____ |
| 8. A trainer takes time to explain why a procedure must be done before employees begin to practice the procedure. | _____ | _____ |

22-D. A company is attempting to determine the effect of laboratory practice on the amount of defective products produced in one of its departments. The company collected the following data on twelve groups of employees who were given varying lengths of practice.

| Employee Group # | Hours of Practice | Average Error Rate (per 1000 pieces) |
|---|---|---|
| 1 | 3 | 16 |
| 2 | 11 | 3 |
| 3 | 7 | 7 |
| 4 | 5 | 7 |
| 5 | 14 | 5 |
| 6 | 3 | 13 |
| 7 | 5 | 5 |
| 8 | 16 | 6 |
| 9 | 10 | 3 |
| 10 | 8 | 9 |
| 11 | 7 | 6 |
| 12 | 4 | 11 |

1. Plot the data on the scattergram below.

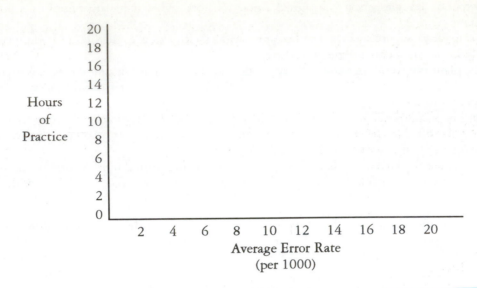

Hours of Practice (y-axis: 0, 2, 4, 6, 8, 10, 12, 14, 16, 18, 20)

Average Error Rate (per 1000) (x-axis: 2, 4, 6, 8, 10, 12, 14, 16, 18, 20)

2. What conclusions can you draw about the relationship between the amount of practice time and error rates in production as a result of reviewing the data from this study?

_____

_____

3. How would you explain the performance of Groups 5 and 8?

_____

_____

4. Based on the study, what would be the ideal amount of practice time to reduce errors as much as possible?

_____

_____

22-E. When a supervisor conducts an evaluation conference with an employee to review the employee's performance, it should be a positive experience. Discussion should focus on the employee's performance, not on the employee. The supervisor should identify ways the employee can improve and what will happen if improvement occurs. The employee should be encouraged to do a good job.

In each of the following examples, an area for employee improvement is identified. Plan how you would talk to the employee about the concern. Then write two or three sentences to describe your plan for dealing with the employee in an informal evaluation conference.

1. An employee responsible for preparing customer invoices has a record of errors in totaling the amounts on the invoices. Each invoice is double-checked before it is mailed, so the errors are found and corrected before they are mailed. Since the employee has a large number of invoices to complete each day, it appears he hurries, knowing someone else will correct the mistakes.

Your plan: _____

_____

_____

2. An employee is responsible for operating a machine that punches holes through metal plates one inch thick. A safety shield is supposed to be lowered in place each time the punch is operated. The employee has found that more plates can be punched if the shield is not used. You know that if the employee's hands are caught in the press, a serious injury will result.

Your plan: _____

_____

_____

3. The employee is having trouble organizing her work. She is very effective when she is organized, but spends a great deal of time finding materials and supplies and determining how she will do the job.

Your plan: _____

_____

_____

4. The employee seems to be very shy around co-workers. He seldom speaks to them, does not sit with them at lunch, and seldom goes on breaks with anyone he works with. It does not seem to affect the quality of the work he does by himself, but he is not as effective when he works with others.

Your plan: _____

_____

_____

22-F. Often, training needs can be identified from the areas where employees are not performing as well as expected. Review each of the four situations in Problem 22-E. For each, identify a specific training need. Then recommend the type of training you believe would be most effective in improving employee performance.

| | Training Need | Recommended Training |
|---|---|---|
| 1 | | |
| 2 | | |
| 3 | | |
| 4 | | |

# CONTINUING PROJECT
## Chapter 22 Activities

The fast food industry is recognizing the importance of well-trained employees to the success of the business. Because of the nature of your business, you will need to emphasize high-quality customer service. Training and evaluation of employees will be an important part of that emphasis.

### Data Collection

1. Through a review of newspapers and magazine articles, or by observing practices in local fast food restaurants, identify five areas in the business where training is needed to improve customer service.
2. Collect samples of employee evaluation forms used in businesses. Review the forms to identify the types of skills being evaluated and the procedures used to complete the evaluation.

### Analysis

1. Describe the type of training you would provide for (a) new employees and (b) experienced employees.
2. List three job skills needed by an employee of your business. For each skill, develop an objective method for evaluating employee performance.

# Study Guide

**Part A**—*Directions:* Indicate your answer to each of the following questions by circling either yes or no in the Answers column.

|  |  | Answers | For Scoring |
|---|---|---|---|
| 1. | Were a number of companies forced to restructure and downsize in the 1980s and 1990s? | yes no | 1. _____ |
| 2. | Is job security the likelihood that a person's employment will not be terminated in the future? | yes no | 2. _____ |
| 3. | Have human resources departments been able to avoid involvement in the reorganization efforts of companies? | yes no | 3. _____ |
| 4. | Is organizational development a term used to describe programs that match the long-term career planning of employees with the employment needs of the business? | yes no | 4. _____ |
| 5. | In the past, did many companies terminate employees who were not needed without considering future employment needs? | yes no | 5. _____ |
| 6. | Does an effective career development program require the involvement of the human resources department, company managers, and employees? | yes no | 6. _____ |
| 7. | Must career paths move an employee from an entry-level position into management? | yes no | 7. _____ |
| 8. | Should each job in a company be a part of a career path? | yes no | 8. _____ |
| 9. | Is a career center another name for an assessment center? | yes no | 9. _____ |
| 10. | Should all of the employees in a company have access to the career development services? | yes no | 10. _____ |
| 11. | Should all of the employees of a company be able to participate in management training? | yes no | 11. _____ |
| 12. | Can a company that does not discriminate in employment practices still have an environment that is not open and supportive for minority employees? | yes no | 12. _____ |
| 13. | Do studies show that employees who are treated well in a company will be more likely to contribute to its success? | yes no | 13. _____ |
| 14. | Is an important objective of organizational development to decrease the importance of work relationships? | yes no | 14. _____ |
| 15. | Do U.S. workers have the right by law to form a union in a company? | yes no | 15. _____ |
| 16. | Has union membership grown rapidly in the past 10 years? | yes no | 16. _____ |
| 17. | Is motivation the reason that cause people to act in a certain way? | yes no | 17. _____ |
| 18. | Are most employees only concerned with the amount of their paycheck and benefits? | yes no | 18. _____ |
| 19. | Is it beneficial for companies to train employees for more than one job in a company even though they typically perform only one? | yes no | 19. _____ |
| 20. | When quality circles are used in companies, are managers eliminated from the decision-making process? | yes no | 20. _____ |

**Part B**—*Directions:* For each of the following statements, select the word, or group of words, that best completes the statement. In the Answers column, write the letter corresponding to the answer selected.

|  | Answers | For Scoring |
|---|---|---|
| 1. A process businesses have used to reorganize work and resources to improve the effectiveness of the organization is known as (a) downsizing, (b) restructuring, (c) layoffs, (d) joint ventures. | _____ | 1. _____ |
| 2. When human resources departments help employees match their long-term employment needs with those of the business, they are involved in (a) organizational development, (b) restructuring, (c) career planning, (d) employee evaluation. | _____ | 2. _____ |
| 3. In the past, the attitude of many companies toward employees was (a) you have a job for life, (b) if you are not needed, you will be terminated, (c) we will only hire part-time employees, (d) we will give you regular promotions. | _____ | 3. _____ |
| 4. Which of the following is needed for an effective career development program? (a) career paths, (b) effective employee evaluation, (c) employee training, (d) all of the responses. | _____ | 4. _____ |
| 5. Traditional career paths moved employees (a) into other companies, (b) into dead-end jobs, (c) toward management positions, (d) into highly technical positions. | _____ | 5. _____ |
| 6. Making employees aware of opportunities and helping them plan career paths is a part of (a) assessment, (b) career counseling, (c) the recruitment and selection process, (d) management development. | _____ | 6. _____ |
| 7. Most companies assign responsibility for organizing and managing career development programs to (a) the CEO, (b) every supervisor, (c) the human resources department, (d) an outside consultant. | _____ | 7. _____ |
| 8. Which of the following is NOT an important federal law regulating relationships between labor unions and management? (a) the Americans with Disabilities Act, (b) the Wagner Act, (c) the Taft-Hartley Act, (d) the Landrum-Griffin Act. | _____ | 8. _____ |
| 9. When employees are encouraged to participate in important decision making in the business, they are involved in (a) cross training, (b) job design, (c) job enrichment, (d) labor relations. | _____ | 9. _____ |
| 10. Companies are finding that employees appreciate being involved in the organization when (a) they see managers being removed from decision making, (b) they have increases in salary and benefits as well, (c) it doesn't take time away from their work, (d) their efforts are recognized by management. | _____ | 10. _____ |

**Part C**—*Directions:* In the Answers column, write the letter of the word or expression in Column I that most closely matches each statement in Column II.

| Column I | Column II | Answers | For Scoring |
|---|---|---|---|
| A. Quality circles<br>B. Give backs<br>C. Boycott<br>D. Lockout<br>E. Strike | 1. Reductions in wages and benefits agreed upon in previous labor contracts. | _____ | 1. _____ |
|  | 2. A decision by union members not to buy the products of a company with which they have a dispute. | _____ | 2. _____ |
|  | 3. Employee teams meet regularly to solve problems and to improve operations. | _____ | 3. _____ |
|  | 4. A temporary work stoppage enforced by the employer. | _____ | 4. _____ |
|  | 5. The refusal of union members to go to work. | _____ | 5. _____ |

**Directions:** Study each controversial issue carefully. Follow the advice of your teacher before listing in the columns provided reasons why people might answer Yes or No. Your teacher may want you to work with a classmate, talk with others in your community to gather information, or use the library to gather facts.

23-1. When employees are regularly involved in decision making through quality circles and similar strategies, is there no longer a need for labor unions?

| Reasons for "Yes" | Reasons for "No" |
| --- | --- |
| | |

23-2. When employees are hired in many Japanese firms, they usually remain with the company for as long as they choose, provided they perform effectively. Should U.S. companies adopt a philosophy like those Japanese firms?

| Reasons for "Yes" | Reasons for "No" |
| --- | --- |
| | |

# PROBLEMS

23-A. Traditional career paths in business have advanced from an entry-level position requiring limited amounts of education and experience to management positions requiring advanced education and experience. Today, new career paths are available allowing those employees who do not choose a career in management to advance into more specialized careers with greater responsibilities.

    Using the classified advertising of a large newspaper, identify four different jobs that you believe would form a traditional career level from entry level to management. Complete the chart on the left with the required information for each job. Then prepare another career ladder with jobs leading to greater responsibility but not management. Complete the chart on the right with the required information.

| Management Career Ladder | Non-management Career Ladder |
|---|---|
| **Beginning Job:**<br><br>  Job title:<br><br>  Major duties:<br><br>  Education:<br><br>  Experience: | **Beginning Job:**<br><br>  Job title:<br><br>  Major duties:<br><br>  Education:<br><br>  Experience: |
| **2nd Level:**<br><br>  Job title:<br><br>  Major duties:<br><br>  Education:<br><br>  Experience: | **2nd Level:**<br><br>  Job title:<br><br>  Major duties:<br><br>  Education:<br><br>  Experience: |
| **3rd Level:**<br><br>  Job title:<br><br>  Major duties:<br><br>  Education:<br><br>  Experience: | **3rd Level:**<br><br>  Job title:<br><br>  Major duties:<br><br>  Education:<br><br>  Experience: |
| **4th Level:**<br><br>  Job title:<br><br>  Major duties:<br><br>  Education:<br><br>  Experience: | **4th Level:**<br><br>  Job title:<br><br>  Major duties:<br><br>  Education:<br><br>  Experience: |

**23-B.** The following chart shows the number of union members and the total number of people employed in the United States for selected years as reported by the U.S. Department of Commerce. Using library research, determine the total labor force and union membership for the most recent year. Then, complete the chart by calculating the union membership as a percentage of the total labor force for each of the years.

| Year | Total Labor Force | Union Membership | % of Total |
|------|-------------------|------------------|------------|
| 1930 | 50,014,705 | 3,401,000 | |
| 1940 | 56,238,709 | 8,717,000 | |
| 1950 | 63,977,578 | 14,267,000 | |
| 1960 | 65,880,000 | 18,117,000 | |
| 1970 | 78,904,942 | 20,752,000 | |
| 1980 | 89,912,280 | 20,500,000 | |
| 1990 | 103,658,536 | 17,000,000 | |
| 19XX | | | |

1. Why do you believe union membership has decreased as a percentage of the total labor force during the past 30 years? _____

_____

_____

_____

_____

_____

2. What changes in our economy do you believe could lead to an increase in union membership in the future?

_____

_____

_____

_____

_____

_____

**23-C.** Many employee/employer relations are regulated by federal laws. For each of the items listed below, indicate whether it is a legal or illegal activity by placing a check mark in the appropriate column.

| | Activity | Legal | Illegal |
|---|---|---|---|
| 1. | Workers in any company covered by federal laws can form a union. ..................... | _____ | _____ |
| 2. | If workers attempt to form a union and the attempt is unsuccessful, the employer can fire those workers who tried to organize the union. ......................................... | _____ | _____ |
| 3. | Where a union exists, management can be required to hire only union members. | _____ | _____ |
| 4. | Unions can protect their members by requiring the company to employ a minimum number of union members for a job, even if that number is not needed to complete the job. ......................................................................................... | _____ | _____ |
| 5. | The President of the United States can stop strikes he does not believe are in the best interest of the country. ......................................................................... | _____ | _____ |
| 6. | Union members have the right to a hearing if management wants to discipline them. ................................................................................................................... | _____ | _____ |
| 7. | Union members can agree to refuse to buy products from a company with which they have a disagreement and encourage others to do the same. ........................... | _____ | _____ |
| 8. | If management is in a dispute with a union, they can actually prevent union members from entering the business to work. .................................................... | _____ | _____ |
| 9. | During a strike, management may hire nonunion members to fill jobs that are held by union members. ........................................................................................ | _____ | _____ |
| 10. | After a contract agreement has been reached to increase wages and benefits, the union and management can negotiate to reduce the employees' salaries and benefits. | _____ | _____ |

**23-D.** The Brunston Co. has just completed a profile of its employees. Findings included:

1. While 14 percent of the general population is made up of minority races, the company has only a 5 percent minority employment level.
2. While women represent 52 percent of the workforce, they perform 83 percent of the clerical jobs and 27 percent of the management jobs.
3. White males earn an average of 6 percent more in wages than minority males in similar jobs; white males also earn 13 percent more than females doing equal work.

What are your reactions to the data presented? What might be some reasons for the employee profile as it

exists? _____

_____

If you were the president of the Brunston Co., what would you do about your future employment practices

based on this data? Write a two paragraph memo to the company's managers to identify the changes you

plan to make. _____

_____

_____

_____

_____

_____

_____

**23-E.** Complete the diagram below by placing the five categories of needs in their appropriate order on the left side of the diagram. Then match the five motivating activities with the most appropriate need and write the activity in the correct space on the right side of the diagram.

**Needs:** Social needs; Self-realization needs; Physical needs; Safety needs; Self-respect needs

**Motivating Activities:**
1. Because of the eyestrain caused by use of video-display terminals, computer operators are given five-minute breaks each hour.
2. The company newsletter features an employee of the month who gives outstanding customer service.
3. After employees have worked for five consecutive months without being late for work, they are put on a flex-time plan and can determine when they will begin and end their work day.
4. The company has formed a volleyball league and each department's employees and supervisors has a team.
5. All new employees are given two weeks of training in a laboratory before they are asked to begin operating the equipment on the assembly line.

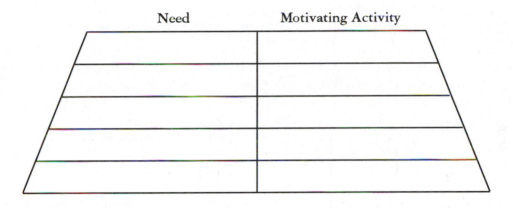

**23-F.** A recent survey was completed of 823 executives whose companies have been using self-directed work teams that are responsible for the day-to-day decisions for their work areas. When asked what were the barriers to developing effective work teams, they listed the following factors:

| Barrier | % of Respondents | No. of Respondents |
|---|---|---|
| Insufficient training | 54% | _____ |
| Supervisor resistance | 47% | _____ |
| Incompatible policies | 47% | _____ |
| Lack of planning | 40% | _____ |
| Lack of management support | 31% | _____ |
| Lack of union support | 24% | _____ |

1. Complete the chart by calculating the number of executives who identified each of the barriers.
2. Prepare one recommendation for managers and one recommendation for employees on what companies should do to increase the chances that self-directed work teams will be effective.

Recommendation to Management: _____

_____

_____

Recommendation to Employees: _____

_____

_____

# CONTINUING PROJECT
## Chapter 23 Activities

It is not likely that you will have direct contact with a union as a new business owner. However, you should be familiar with unions operating in your area and understand their objectives. You also must begin to determine how you will respond to employees' needs as your business grows.

### Data Collection

1. Identify unions that operate in your community. Also identify the national unions that represent employees in restaurants and other types of food-service businesses.

2. Read newspaper and magazine articles on employee-management relations. Identify business practices described in the articles that appear to have a negative effect on those relations and practices that appear to have a positive effect.

### Analysis

1. Prepare a career development plan that you will follow to prepare for the responsibilities of starting and operating your own business. Identify sources of formal and informal training available to small business owners in your community or area.

2. Develop a list of employment practices and management procedures for use in your business designed to encourage effective management-employee relations.

<table>
<tr><td rowspan="3">Chapter 24<br><br>Management Functions and Decision Making</td><td rowspan="3">Name _____<br><br><br>Date _____</td><td colspan="5" align="center">Scoring Record</td></tr>
<tr><td></td><td>Part A</td><td>Part B</td><td>Part C</td><td>Total</td></tr>
<tr><td>Perfect score</td><td>20</td><td>10</td><td>5</td><td>35</td></tr>
<tr><td colspan="2">My score</td><td></td><td></td><td></td><td></td></tr>
</table>

# Study Guide

**Part A**—*Directions:* Indicate your answer to each of the following questions by circling either yes or no in the Answers column.

|  |  | Answers | For Scoring |
|--|--|--|--|
| 1. | Will most people who want to become managers start their management careers as supervisors? | yes no | 1. _____ |
| 2. | Are managers responsible for the success or failure of a company? | yes no | 2. _____ |
| 3. | Is the primary work of all managers grouped within six functions? | yes no | 3. _____ |
| 4. | Do many employees of a business complete activities that could be considered management activities? | yes no | 4. _____ |
| 5. | Would an experienced employee who is given the responsibility to be the leader of a group project be classified as a manager? | yes no | 5. _____ |
| 6. | In order to be a manager, does a person have to complete all of the management functions and have authority over other jobs and people? | yes no | 6. _____ |
| 7. | Do most supervisors spend all of their time on management activities? | yes no | 7. _____ |
| 8. | Do a manager's responsibilities remain the same even as he or she is promoted in the organization? | yes no | 8. _____ |
| 9. | Are most supervisors promoted into management in the same area in which they have worked? | yes no | 9. _____ |
| 10. | Should supervisors be more concerned about the individual goals of their employees rather than the goals of the business? | yes no | 10. _____ |
| 11. | Do most employees prefer to work for supervisors who are interested in them and their ideas? | yes no | 11. _____ |
| 12. | Can a supervisor contribute to the profitability of the company by controlling costs in the area where he or she works? | yes no | 12. _____ |
| 13. | Is a work schedule an important tool for supervisors to use in daily planning? | yes no | 13. _____ |
| 14. | Is much of the communication between supervisors and their employees done orally? | yes no | 14. _____ |
| 15. | Should most supervisors spend more time on non-managerial activities and less time on management functions? | yes no | 15. _____ |
| 16. | Does every company, whether it is small or large, need a management information system as an important management tool? | yes no | 16. _____ |
| 17. | When managers use a management information system do they spend more time on controlling activities? | yes no | 17. _____ |
| 18. | Should a business actually conduct all of the research it needs for management decision making? | yes no | 18. _____ |
| 19. | Do the terms "problem" and "symptom" mean essentially the same thing? | yes no | 19. _____ |
| 20. | Once a solution to a problem is implemented in a company, should a manager avoid changing the solution even if evidence suggests it is not working well? | yes no | 20. _____ |

**Part B**—*Directions:* For each of the following statements, select the word, or group of words, that best completes the statement. In the Answers column, write the letter corresponding to the answer selected.

|  | Answers | For Scoring |
|---|---|---|

1. Employees will be most successful when they move into a management position if (a) they have worked for a poor supervisor so they know what not to do, (b) they begin work as a supervisor before receiving training, (c) they have the chance to try supervision before making a final decision, (d) all of the responses.  _____  1. _____

2. Which of the following is most likely to complete all of the management functions? (a) a small business owner, (b) the top executive of a multinational corporation, (c) a middle manager, (d) all of the responses. ....................................  _____  2. _____

3. A top-level manager who spends most of the time on management functions is (a) an executive, (b) a mid-manager, (c) a supervisor, (d) a team leader. ..........  _____  3. _____

4. The type of manager who works most directly with employees on a daily basis is (a) an executive (b) a mid-manager, (c) a supervisor, (d) none of the responses.  _____  4. _____

5. Which of the following is NOT one of the common responsibilities of supervisors? (a) communicating goals and directions, (b) motivating employees to work effectively, (c) keeping management informed of employee ideas and concerns, (d) developing long-range plans for the organization. ....................................  _____  5. _____

6. Which of the following activities of supervisors relates most directly to quality control? (a) developing work schedules, (b) developing and checking standards, (c) using effective listening skills, (d) setting priorities so the most important work is done. ................................................................  _____  6. _____

7. Standards that are not being met and the amount of difference between a standard and actual performance are identified in (a) a job description, (b) a performance evaluation, (c) a variance report, (d) all of the responses. ....................  _____  7. _____

8. A difficult situation requiring a solution is (a) a problem, (b) a symptom, (c) a standard, (d) an alternative. ................................................................  _____  8. _____

9. Which of the following steps in problem solving is in the correct order? (a) analyze solutions, identify the problem; (b) determine possible solutions, identify the problem; (c) analyze solutions, select the best solution; (d) all of the responses. ................................................................  _____  9. _____

10. Which of the following would NOT be appropriate in selecting the solution to be implemented to solve an important problem? (a) Take time rather than making a quick decision. (b) Involve others to help with the decision. (c) Select the least expensive solution. (d) All of the responses. ..........................................  _____  10. _____

**Part C**—*Directions:* In the Answers column, write the letter of the word or expression in Column I that most closely matches each statement in Column II.

| Column I | Column II | Answers | For Scoring |
|---|---|---|---|
| A. Planning<br>B. Organizing<br>C. Implementing<br>D. Controlling<br>E. Management | 1. Accomplishing the goals of an organization through the effective use of people and other resources. ...................................... | _____ | 1. _____ |
|  | 2. Determining how plans can most effectively be accomplished and arranging resources to complete work. ........................................... | _____ | 2. _____ |
|  | 3. Evaluating results to determine if the company's objectives have been accomplished as planned. | _____ | 3. _____ |
|  | 4. Analyzing information and making decisions about what needs to be done. ...................... | _____ | 4. _____ |
|  | 5. Carrying out the plans and helping employees to work effectively. ...................................... | _____ | 5. _____ |

**Directions:** Study each controversial issue carefully. Follow the advice of your teacher before listing in the columns provided reasons why people might answer Yes or No. Your teacher may want you to work with a classmate, talk with others in your community to gather information, or use the library to gather facts.

24-1. Since supervisors are responsible for the day-to-day operations of a business, are they more important to the success of the business than executives who are responsible for long-range planning and direction of the business?

| Reasons for "Yes" | Reasons for "No" |
| --- | --- |
|  |  |

24-2. Should supervisors be selected from those employees who are the top performers in their areas or should they be selected from those who have abilities to work well with and motivate other employees?

| Reasons for "Yes" | Reasons for "No" |
| --- | --- |
|  |  |

# PROBLEMS

**24-A.** There are four functions that all managers perform: planning, organizing, implementing, and controlling. While each manager completes all functions, managers at different levels in a business spend more time on some functions than others. In one company, the information was collected on the average number of hours spent by executives, mid-managers, and supervisors each week completing each of the functions. The results are:

|  | Planning | Organizing | Implementing | Controlling |
|---|---|---|---|---|
| Executives | 24 | 15 | 12 | 8 |
| Mid-managers | 17 | 15 | 19 | 14 |
| Supervisors | 6 | 10 | 16 | 12 |

Complete the following figure by shading in the appropriate sections representing the percentage of work time spent by each group of managers during the week.

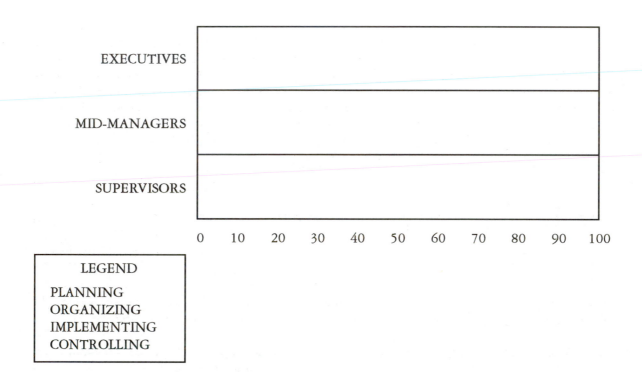

24-B. For each of the following management activities, identify which of the four management functions is being completed. Place the letter of the correct function in the blank beside the item number:

P = Planning
O = Organizing
I = Implementing
C = Controlling

_____ 1. Determining the types of raw materials to use in order to develop a high-quality product.

_____ 2. Completing an employee performance appraisal.

_____ 3. Dividing a large sales territory into two smaller territories and assigning managers and salespeople to the territory.

_____ 4. Deciding if a new product should be added after reviewing test-market results.

_____ 5. Discussing a problem with two employees to encourage them to work more closely together rather than continuing to have conflicts.

_____ 6. Reviewing the financial statements for the past six months.

_____ 7. Deciding to hire an advertising agency to promote a new product because the promotion manager is currently overworked.

_____ 8. Conducting a department meeting.

_____ 9. Determining salary increases based on annual performance evaluations.

_____10. Deciding whether to sell stock in the company or borrow money in order to finance a new building.

**24-C.** You have learned that while supervisors from various companies have many differences in their jobs they still have a common set of responsibilities. Those common responsibilities are listed in the left column of the following chart. Locate a newspaper that has a large section of classified advertisements for employment. Identify several job announcements for supervisors. Use those advertisements to complete the remaining columns of the chart. For each of the responsibilities listed, (1) identify a part of the job description from one of the advertisements that relates to that responsibility and copy the statement into the second column; (2) copy the job title for that position in the third column; (3) write the name of the company offering the position in the fourth column; and (4) identify the type of business (manufacturer, retailer, etc.) in the last column. Try to identify a different job and company for each of the supervisor responsibilities.

| Supervisor responsibility | Job description | Job title | Company | Type of Business |
|---|---|---|---|---|
| Communicate goals and directions | | | | |
| Keep management informed | | | | |
| Improve employee performance | | | | |
| Motivate employees | | | | |
| Use resources efficiently | | | | |

**24-D.** A just-in-time inventory system is used to keep inventory levels as low as possible to save costs of storing the inventory. The system is organized to anticipate the number of days it takes to order materials and have them delivered to the factory. Effective management information is essential to make accurate decisions. Use the information in each of the following problems to manage a just-in-time inventory system.

1. Production rate: 20 units of the materials are used in production each day
   Order processing time: 4 days
   Delivery time: 8 days
   How many units of materials should be left in inventory on the day that an order is placed?

   _____

2. Production rate: 10 tons of materials are used in production each day
   Order processing time: 14 days
   Delivery time: 10 days
   If the inventory level will be at 0 on July 16, when should an order be placed in order for a new supply to arrive by the 16th?

   _____

3. Order processing time: 5 days
   Delivery time: 11 days
   Units of material in inventory on the day the order is placed: 880 units
   How many units of materials are used in production each day?

   _____

**24-E.** In preparation for the end-of-year selling season, the owner of a small gift shop invested $45,000 in inventory. At the end of the year, an analysis of sales records showed the following results.

| | |
|---|---|
| Sales at retail: | $99,500 |
| Sales at cost: | 39,800 |
| Merchandise returned (cannot be resold): | 675 |
| Merchandise damaged: | 900 |
| Merchandise used in promotions: | 225 |
| Remaining inventory: | 700 |

1. Using the figures above, calculate the amount of inventory unaccounted for by the sales records.

   _____

2. Offer an explanation for the variance between the amount of inventory that should be remaining and the

   actual remaining inventory. _____

   _____

   _____

3. Would the variance between the expected and actual inventory be a symptom or a problem? _____

4. Would the answer you gave to question #2 be a symptom or a problem? _____

5. Calculate the percentage of the inventory variance compared to retail sales. _____

**24-F.** Use the information from Problem 24-E to complete this problem.

1. List two symptoms of a potential problem facing the business suggested from the information.

   a. Symptom: _____

   b. Symptom: _____

2. Identify a potential problem the company needs to solve to improve the sales performance or inventory control.

   Problem: _____

3. List the steps the owner should take to solve the problem.

   _____

   _____

   _____

   _____

   _____

   _____

# CONTINUING PROJECT
## Chapter 24 Activities

There is a very high failure rate for new small businesses. One of the major reasons for failure is that the owner does not practice effective **management** skills. As an owner, you must devote adequate time to management and complete all major management functions.

### Data Collection

1. Survey five managers of small businesses. Ask them to estimate the amount of time they spend on each of the four management functions. Summarize the results.
2. Identify several problems that you will probably face in operating your business. Complete the steps in problem solving to develop an appropriate solution. As you analyze possible solutions, identify several sources of useful information, including business research.

### Analysis

1. Develop a chart with four headings: planning, organizing, implementing, and controlling. Under each heading, list the activities you need to complete to manage your business effectively.
2. Under the list of activities developed above, estimate (a) how much time you will need to devote to each activity and (b) when each activity during a typical month will be completed. Then develop a sample monthly calendar on which you schedule management activities.
3. For each of the problems identified in the data collection section above, select the solution you believe is likely to be most effective. Then develop a set of procedures to be followed in accomplishing each solution.

# Study Guide

**Part A**—*Directions:* Indicate your answer to each of the following questions by circling either yes or no in the Answers column.

| | | Answers | | For Scoring |
|---|---|---|---|---|
| 1. | Do the people who are responsible for an organization need to have leadership skills in order for the organization to be effective? ..................................... | yes | no | 1. _____ |
| 2. | Do managers today have total authority over the employees in a business? ..... | yes | no | 2. _____ |
| 3. | Does human relations refer to how well people get along together? ............... | yes | no | 3. _____ |
| 4. | Can supervisors get by without leadership skills since they are at the lowest level of management? ..................................................................................... | yes | no | 4. _____ |
| 5. | Is dependability an important leadership characteristic? ................................. | yes | no | 5. _____ |
| 6. | Do effective leaders encourage others to share their ideas, experiences, and opinions? ........................................................................................................ | yes | no | 6. _____ |
| 7. | If a manager is able to get others to do what he or she wants, is that manager an effective leader? ........................................................................................... | yes | no | 7. _____ |
| 8. | Is position power based on the ability to control resources, rewards, and punishments? .......................................................................................................... | yes | no | 8. _____ |
| 9. | Can a person have power because others identify with and want to be accepted by him or her? ............................................................................................... | yes | no | 9. _____ |
| 10. | Are managers the only people who have power in an organization? ............... | yes | no | 10. _____ |
| 11. | Are many managers hired and evaluated on the basis of leadership characteristics? .......................................................................................................... | yes | no | 11. _____ |
| 12. | Are human relations skills among the easiest business skills to develop? ........ | yes | no | 12. _____ |
| 13. | Should managers treat all employees in the same way? ................................. | yes | no | 13. _____ |
| 14. | Should managers attempt to match job tasks with the needs and interests of employees? ...................................................................................................... | yes | no | 14. _____ |
| 15. | Have studies found that, in general, all employees enjoy their work and get satisfaction from a job well done? .................................................................... | yes | no | 15. _____ |
| 16. | Is an autocratic style of leadership most effective when efficiency is important? | yes | no | 16. _____ |
| 17. | Will managers who use a democratic style of leadership generally take more time to make a decision than if another style is used? ................................... | yes | no | 17. _____ |
| 18. | Will the open style of leadership work best with inexperienced employees? ... | yes | no | 18. _____ |
| 19. | Do most management training programs prepare managers to deal with difficult personal problems of their employees? ................................................... | yes | no | 19. _____ |
| 20. | Should managers treat similar violations of work rules consistently? .............. | yes | no | 20. _____ |

|  | Answers | For Scoring |
|---|---|---|

1. The ability to influence individuals and groups to achieve organizational goals is (a) management, (b) human relations, (c) leadership, (d) none of the responses. _____ 1._____

2. When leaders have ambition and persistence in reaching goals, they are demonstrating (a) cooperation, (b) initiative, (c) objectivity, (d) stability. _____ 2._____

3. The ability to control behavior in an organization is known as (a) power, (b) leadership, (c) rewards, (d) cooperation. _____ 3._____

4. Expert power is given to people who (a) hold management positions in an organization, (b) are considered the most knowledgeable, (c) with whom others identify, (d) all of the responses. _____ 4._____

5. The two types of power given to managers by their employees are (a) position and reward, (b) autocratic and democratic, (c) human relations and leadership, (d) expert and identity. _____ 5._____

6. Which of the following is NOT an important human relations skill needed by managers? (a) self-understanding, (b) communication, (c) developing job satisfaction, (d) judgment. _____ 6._____

7. Managers who are able to get people to work well together to accomplish the goals of an organization are using which human relations skill? (a) leadership, (b) group building, (c) power, (d) authority. _____ 7._____

8. Managers who believe employees dislike work are more likely to (a) give employees more responsibility, (b) be effective leaders, (c) use closer supervision and control, (d) have little concern for the quality of employees' work. _____ 8._____

9. Which of the following is a leadership characteristic employees prefer in their managers? (a) encourages employee participation and questions, (b) informs employees of information only when they need to know, (c) implements few changes, (d) keeps employee training to a minimum. _____ 9._____

10. If a business does not have a formal set of work rules, (a) a union will likely be organized, (b) employees will be highly motivated, (c) managers will receive greater respect from employees, (d) each manager should develop his or her own set of procedures and policies. _____ 10._____

**Part C**—*Directions:* In the Answers column, write the letter of the word or expression in Column I that most closely matches each statement in Column II.

| Column I | Column II | Answers | For Scoring |
|---|---|---|---|
| A. Open leader | 1. Encourages workers to share in making decisions about work-related problems. | _____ | 1._____ |
| B. Democratic leader | 2. An employee's boss can give directions and expect the employee to complete the work. | _____ | 2._____ |
| C. Autocratic leader | 3. The ability to influence individuals and groups to achieve organizational goals. | _____ | 3._____ |
| D. Leadership | 4. Gives direct, clear, and precise orders with detailed instructions. | _____ | 4._____ |
| E. Position power | 5. Gives little or no direction to others. | _____ | 5._____ |

**Directions:** Study each controversial issue carefully. Follow the advice of your teacher before listing in the columns provided reasons why people might answer Yes or No. Your teacher may want you to work with a classmate, talk with others in your community to gather information, or use the library to gather facts.

25-1. Do all managers in an organization need effective leadership skills in order for the organization to be successful?

| Reasons for "Yes" | Reasons for "No" |
| --- | --- |
|  |  |

25-2. Do you believe some people are "natural leaders"? That is, they do not need leadership training while other people will never be leaders no matter how much training they receive.

| Reasons for "Yes" | Reasons for "No" |
| --- | --- |
|  |  |

# PROBLEMS

**25-A.** Studies of leaders have found that most effective leaders share common personal characteristics. It is possible to determine if you have those characteristics and to develop a personal plan to improve those characteristics that are not as strong as you would like. You can evaluate your leadership characteristics by answering the following questions. Questions that are answered "yes" or "usually" indicate areas where you already have developed leadership skills. The areas where you answer "sometimes" or "never" indicate traits you will need to improve if you are to become a more effective leader.

| | Always | Usually | Sometimes | Never |
|---|---|---|---|---|
| 1. Do you perform above average in your classes in school? .... | ____ | ____ | ____ | ____ |
| 2. Do you enjoy making decisions? ........................... | ____ | ____ | ____ | ____ |
| 3. Do your parents and friends trust your judgment? ............. | ____ | ____ | ____ | ____ |
| 4. Are you able to put your personal feelings aside when you have to make important decisions? ........................ | ____ | ____ | ____ | ____ |
| 5. Do you take time to gather information before you draw conclusions? ................................................. | ____ | ____ | ____ | ____ |
| 6. Do you look forward to starting new tasks? ................... | ____ | ____ | ____ | ____ |
| 7. When you face a challenge, do you keep working until you find a solution? .............................................. | ____ | ____ | ____ | ____ |
| 8. Can people depend on you to do what you say you will do? | ____ | ____ | ____ | ____ |
| 9. Are you involved in team sports and group activities? ....... | ____ | ____ | ____ | ____ |
| 10. Do you prefer working with others rather than alone? ....... | ____ | ____ | ____ | ____ |
| 11. Are you upset when you see others being dishonest? .......... | ____ | ____ | ____ | ____ |
| 12. Are you willing to say no to your friends when they ask you to do things you disagree with? ............................ | ____ | ____ | ____ | ____ |
| 13. Do you prefer to find new ways to do routine activities rather than continuing to do them the same way? ............. | ____ | ____ | ____ | ____ |
| 14. When you have to do something you have never done before, do you believe you will be successful? ................... | ____ | ____ | ____ | ____ |
| 15. When you are in a difficult situation, do you remain calm? ... | ____ | ____ | ____ | ____ |
| 16. Do you listen to the concerns and problems of your friends more often than you tell them about yourself? ................. | ____ | ____ | ____ | ____ |
| 17. When working in a group, do you encourage everyone to participate and contribute? ............................... | ____ | ____ | ____ | ____ |
| 18. Do you have friends who have different backgrounds and interests than you? .................................... | ____ | ____ | ____ | ____ |
| 19. Do you respect the feelings and beliefs of others, even if you do not agree with them? ................................ | ____ | ____ | ____ | ____ |
| 20. When you are in situations where you don't know other people, do you take the initiative to get to know them? ..... | ____ | ____ | ____ | ____ |

**25-B.** For each of the following items, indicate whether the manager was using an autocratic, democratic, or open style of leadership by placing a check mark in the appropriate column.

| | Autocratic | Democratic | Open |
|---|---|---|---|
| 1. Each worker is allowed to decide how his or her job will be done. ............................................... | ____ | ____ | ____ |
| 2. An employee meeting is held each week to discuss problems. .. | ____ | ____ | ____ |
| 3. The manager lets employees cooperatively decide when breaks should be scheduled. ........................... | ____ | ____ | ____ |
| 4. There are no work rules for the department............. | ____ | ____ | ____ |
| 5. Before changing an evaluation system, the manager told the employees why it was being changed........................ | ____ | ____ | ____ |

208

| | Autocratic | Democratic | Open |
|---|---|---|---|
| 6. The manager tells each new employee how the job should be done. ................................................................... | _____ | _____ | _____ |
| 7. When two employees had an argument, the manager told them how to solve their problem. .......................................... | _____ | _____ | _____ |
| 8. The store owner lets department managers order any merchandise they choose. ............................................. | _____ | _____ | _____ |
| 9. The store owner sets all department budgets. ......................... | _____ | _____ | _____ |
| 10. The manager conducts a brainstorming session to develop a new advertising slogan. ...................................... | _____ | _____ | _____ |

**25-C.** The marketing manager for a manufacturing firm has been given the task to select new automobiles for ten of the company's salespeople. The company has lease agreements with dealers representing three brands of automobiles. The manager knows that each salesperson has personal preferences about the brand, model, and options in an automobile. The company also will save money if all of the cars are leased from the same dealer and even more money if all cars are the same model with the same options.

For each of the three leadership styles, identify how the manager would make the decision on the automobiles to purchase and one advantage and one disadvantage of the use of that style.

**Autocratic Style:** _____

_____

Advantage: _____

_____

Disadvantage: _____

_____

**Democratic Style:** _____

_____

Advantage: _____

_____

Disadvantage: _____

_____

**Open Style:** _____

_____

Advantage: _____

_____

Disadvantage: _____

_____

**25-D.** A recent survey of 150 employees with five or more years of experience asked the employees to identify the type of leadership style they preferred from their supervisors. The following results were obtained:

autocratic—38 employees; democratic—66 employees; open—22 employees; a combination of styles—24 employees.

1. In the space below, construct a pie chart showing the percentage of employees preferring each type of leadership style.

**Employees' Preferred Leadership Styles**

2. In the space below, identify the leadership style you would prefer from a supervisor and the reasons for your preference. _____

_____

_____

_____

3. Why do you believe employees prefer very different leadership styles? How can a manager respond when his or her employees work best under different leadership styles? _____

_____

_____

_____

_____

**25-E.** Work rules are developed to create and maintain an effective work environment and to help employees work efficiently. In the space below, write two work rules for you and the other students in your class. Also write a sentence that describes why you believe the rule would result in an effective work atmosphere in the class and would help students work more efficiently. When your statements have been developed, the other students in the class will vote on each statement. The vote will determine whether they agree that each of your rules would help to maintain an effective and efficient working atmosphere.

**Work Rule #1:** _____

_____

_____

Justification: _____

_____

_____

Student Vote: Agree _____ Disagree _____

**Work Rule #2:** _____

_____

_____

Justification: _____

_____

_____

Student Vote: Agree _____ Disagree _____

# CONTINUING PROJECT
## Chapter 25 Activities

If your business is successful, you may want to expand by purchasing additional food stands to serve more locations at one time. As you add more employees, you will need to provide effective leadership to ensure that they will do an effective job. The activities in this chapter allow you to study your leadership style and to develop necessary work rules for your expanding business.

### Data Collection

1. Write brief descriptions of each of the three leadership styles on a piece of paper. Give the sheet of paper to several of your family members, teachers, or close friends. Ask them to identify the description that best describes the way you work with people.
2. Summarize their responses to see if you have a clear-cut leadership style. Do you agree with the responses?

### Analysis

1. Identify five situations in your business where employees may be required to make decisions. For each situation, identify whether you would use an autocratic, democratic, or open style of leadership to help them with the decision.
2. Develop a list of work rules for the employees of your business. Be certain to consider rules on attendance, hours of work, grooming, care of equipment, safety, and the handling of cash as well as other important areas of employee responsibility.

## Study Guide

**Part A**—*Directions:* Indicate your answer to each of the following questions by circling either yes or no in the Answers column.

| | Answers | For Scoring |
|---|---|---|
| 1. Should a business plan include a detailed financial analysis showing the potential profitability of the firm? | yes no | 1. _____ |
| 2. Are all business managers involved in planning in some way? | yes no | 2. _____ |
| 3. Is planning probably the most important management activity? | yes no | 3. _____ |
| 4. Does planning usually result in more communications and coordination problems in the business? | yes no | 4. _____ |
| 5. Is long-term planning that provides broad goals and directions for the entire business known as operational planning? | yes no | 5. _____ |
| 6. Is the development of a business plan an example of strategic planning? | yes no | 6. _____ |
| 7. Is external analysis the first step in strategic planning? | yes no | 7. _____ |
| 8. Are supervisors usually responsible for strategic planning? | yes no | 8. _____ |
| 9. Are decisions about the resources that will be needed to get the work done in a specific area of the business a part of operational planning? | yes no | 9. _____ |
| 10. Do goals provide the direction for a business? | yes no | 10. _____ |
| 11. Is it better for goals to be general rather than specific? | yes no | 11. _____ |
| 12. Does a schedule include both the identification of tasks to be completed and the time needed to complete each task? | yes no | 12. _____ |
| 13. Is a schedule a yardstick or measure by which something is judged? | yes no | 13. _____ |
| 14. Is a policy more specific than a procedure? | yes no | 14. _____ |
| 15. Does an organizational chart explain where and how employees fit into the company? | yes no | 15. _____ |
| 16. As a business grows, do the number of major divisions in the organization usually decrease? | yes no | 16. _____ |
| 17. Is authority the obligation to do an assigned task? | yes no | 17. _____ |
| 18. In an effective organization, do most employees have more than one supervisor from which to receive job assignments? | yes no | 18. _____ |
| 19. In general, is the span of control larger at the lower levels of an organization than at the higher levels? | yes no | 19. _____ |
| 20. Is the most flexible type of organizational structure the project (matrix) organization? | yes no | 20. _____ |

**Part B**—*Directions:* For each of the following statements, select the word, or group of words, that best completes the statement. In the Answers column, write the letter corresponding to the answer selected.

|  | Answers | For Scoring |
|---|---|---|

1. Which of the following would NOT be a part of strategic planning? (a) mission, (b) goals, (c) strategies, (d) department work assignments. ..................... _____   1. _____

2. To be effective, goals should be (a) general rather than specific, (b) slightly higher than can be realistically achieved, (c) independent from all other goals, (d) none of the responses. .................................................................. _____   2. _____

3. The most widely used planning tool is (a) goals, (b) budgets, (c) standards, (d) schedules. ................................................................................. _____   3. _____

4. Guidelines used in making decisions regarding specific recurring situations are known as (a) policies, (b) procedures, (c) standards, (d) goals. ......................... _____   4. _____

5. The management function responsible for arranging resources and relationships between departments and employees and defining the responsibility each has for accomplishing the job is (a) planning, (b) organizing, (c) implementing, (d) controlling. ............................................................................... _____   5. _____

6. A visual device that shows the structure of an organization and the relationships among workers and divisions of work is (a) a schedule, (b) a strategic plan, (c) an organizational chart, (d) an operational plan. ........................................ _____   6. _____

7. Companies that have started using work teams and that involve employees in planning and decision making have found that span of control (a) must be decreased, (b) can be increased, (c) is no longer needed, (d) is not affected. ...... _____   7. _____

8. The organization in which all authority and responsibility can be traced directly from the top executive to the lowest employee level in an organization is the (a) line organization, (b) line-and-staff organization, (c) matrix organization, (c) decentralized organization. ................................................ _____   8. _____

9. Specialists are available to give advice and assistance to managers in the (a) line organization, (b) line-and-staff organization, (c) matrix organization, (c) decentralized organization. ........................................................... _____   9. _____

10. Managers are given almost total responsibility and authority for the operation of their units in a (a) line organization, (b) line-and-staff organization, (c) centralized organization, (d) decentralized organization. ..................................... _____   10. _____

**Part C**—*Directions:* Complete each sentence by filling in the missing word or words.

| | For Scoring |
|---|---|

1. _____ to make decisions about work assignments is delegated from the _____ to the _____ of an organization. .......................................   1. _____

2. Accountability is the term used to relate each individual's _____ to a superior in the organization for the _____ and _____ of work performed. ...............   2. _____

3. _____ ____ _____ requires that no employee have more than one supervisor at a time. ................................................   3. _____

4. Span of control refers to the _____ of employees who are directly _____ by one person. ................................................   4. _____

5. In a project or matrix organization, _____ _____ are organized to complete a specific project and a project _____ with authority and responsibility for the project is identified. .........................   5. _____

214

**Directions:** Study each controversial issue carefully. Follow the advice of your teacher before listing in the columns provided reasons why people might answer Yes or No. Your teacher may want you to work with a classmate, talk with others in your community to gather information, or use the library to gather facts.

26-1. Do you believe that long-range plans should be developed in businesses where economic conditions and competition are changing very rapidly?

| Reasons for "Yes" | Reasons for "No" |
| --- | --- |
|  |  |

26-2. Do you believe most businesses would be more successful if they used a project or matrix organizational plan rather than a line or a line-and-staff organizational plan?

| Reasons for "Yes" | Reasons for "No" |
| --- | --- |
|  |  |

# PROBLEMS

**26-A.** Classify each of the following activities of a business as either strategic planning or operational planning by placing a check mark in the appropriate column.

| Business Activity | Strategic Planning | Operational Planning |
|---|---|---|
| 1. A new warehouse will be built to serve the markets in the northeast section of the country. | ⎯ | ⎯ |
| 2. The advertising budget for the next three months will be increased by 2 percent to attract more customers into the store. | ⎯ | ⎯ |
| 3. The Cleveland facility will schedule a one-week shut-down in December to allow equipment repairs. | ⎯ | ⎯ |
| 4. An export office in Rome will be used to develop plans for European market development. | ⎯ | ⎯ |
| 5. A small business owner decides to expand into other states by selling franchises. | ⎯ | ⎯ |
| 6. Employees will be asked to work three hours of overtime each week to meet the increased summer demand. | ⎯ | ⎯ |

**26-B.** As a manager of a printing department you are responsible for scheduling the time of three employees. Each employee works from 9 a.m. until 5 p.m., with lunch from 12:00 until 1:00. You have the following jobs that can be assigned to your employees. All jobs do not have to be assigned.

Job 1—2 hours to complete—must be completed today.
Job 2—3 1/2 hours to complete—can be completed tomorrow.
Job 3—5 1/2 hours to complete—must be completed today.
Job 4—1 1/2 hours to complete—must be completed today.
Job 5—3 hours to complete—can be completed tomorrow; cannot be divided.
Job 6—4 hours to complete—must be completed today.
Job 7—3 hours to complete—must be completed today.
Job 8—2 1/2 hours to complete—must be completed today.
Job 9—4 hours to complete—can be completed tomorrow.
Job 10—2 hours to complete—can be completed tomorrow; cannot be divided.

Using the following form, assign the jobs to your three employees. You must make certain that jobs 1, 3, 4, 6, 7, and 8 are done today. Employees should be busy all day, but they cannot begin a job that cannot be completed before 5 p.m. if it is noted that the job cannot be divided.

| Employee | 9:00 | 10:00 | 11:00 | 12:00 | 1:00 | 2:00 | 3:00 | 4:00 | 5:00 |
|---|---|---|---|---|---|---|---|---|---|
| O'Brien | | | | Lunch | | | | | |
| Jacobs | | | | Lunch | | | | | |
| Stein | | | | Lunch | | | | | |

216

**26-C.** Business goals must be specific and meaningful in order to be useful to managers and employers. Each of the following statements is very general, but can be used as a basis for developing a **goal** for the business. Rewrite each statement to make it an effective goal.

1. The men's shoe department needs an increased sales volume.

   _____

2. Too many radios produced on the third shift are defective and have to be discarded.

   _____

3. We've seen an increase in employee turnover since January.

   _____

4. We would like to increase the amount each customer spends when they shop in our Westgate store.

   _____

**26-D.** A well-developed outline of procedures for completing a task can be an effective tool to help a new employee learn a job. However, it is not easy to develop procedures and include every necessary step. In the space below, outline the procedures someone should follow in accurately writing a check. To determine if the procedures are correct, have another student follow the procedures exactly to fill in the check blank. When the student is finished, evaluate the work to see if it has been done correctly.

_____

_____

_____

_____

_____

_____

**N.E. Name**
**33 Your Street**
**Anytown, U.S. 11223**

\# _____

_____ 19 _____   72-7073/2739

PAY TO THE
ORDER OF _____   $ _____

_____ D O L L A R S

**THE FIRST NATIONAL BANK**
**ANYTOWN, U.S. 11223**

MEMO _____   _____

⑈27390734⑈

26-E. The most common type of organization in a large business is line-and-staff. In such an organization, the staff person investigates problems and consults with and advises line administrators. The line administrators determine policies and procedures and give orders for carrying out their decisions.

The chart below describes ten positions within a company, whether they are line or staff positions, and their responsibilities. After reviewing the information, draw a line-and-staff organizational chart on the next page showing the relationships between the ten positions.

| | Position | Line or Staff | Responsibilities |
|---|---|---|---|
| 1. | President | line | Directs the company |
| 2. | Vice president of manufacturing | line | Reports to president |
| 3. | Company attorney | staff | Advises president and vice president of manufacturing and sales |
| 4. | Chemist who tests raw materials purchased | staff | Works with production management |
| 5. | District sales manager | line | Reports to vice president of sales |
| 6. | Advertising specialist | staff | Works with sales personnel |
| 7. | Supervisor of production | line | Reports to superintendent of manufacturing |
| 8. | Vice president of sales | line | Reports to president |
| 9. | Personnel manager | staff | Works with president and vice presidents of manufacturing and sales |
| 10. | Superintendent of manufacturing | line | Reports to vice president of manufacturing |

# Line-and-Staff Organizational Chart

# CONTINUING PROJECT
## Chapter 26 Activities

A new business owner will spend the majority of time on planning and organizing activities. Starting with a business plan, the owner must develop goals, budgets, schedules, policies, and procedures. As employees are added, decisions must be made on how to organize and divide work so it will be completed effectively. This chapter will study the planning and organizing functions of management.

### Data Collection

1. Meet with a successful small business manager and discuss the importance of planning, how the business manager plans for the business, and the types of planning tools used.
2. Read several magazine articles on ways that businesses are reorganizing work for more effective operations. Summarize the key points from those articles that you believe are useful to small businesses.

### Analysis

1. Divide a sheet of paper into two columns. Label one column "strategic planning" and the other "operational planning." List as many areas as you can under each label for your business.
2. For each of the planning tools listed in Chapter 26, identify how you will use the tool and when each needs to be completed in your business.
3. Assume you have added four part-time employees to help you operate your business. One person is identified as the assistant manager. Prepare an organizational chart for the business in which job titles and duties are listed for each employee.

# Study Guide

**Part A**—*Directions:* Indicate your answer to each of the following questions by circling either yes or no in the Answers column.

| | | Answers | For Scoring |
|---|---|---|---|
| 1. | Are plans likely to be ineffective if they are not implemented well? .............. | yes no | 1. _____ |
| 2. | Do the terms implementing and directing mean essentially the same thing as they relate to business management? ........................................................ | yes no | 2. _____ |
| 3. | Is employee motivation influenced by both internal and external factors? ...... | yes no | 3. _____ |
| 4. | Is there a positive relationship between need satisfaction of an employee and motivation? ........................................................................................... | yes no | 4. _____ |
| 5. | Will each member of a work team usually be working to achieve very different goals? ................................................................................................... | yes no | 5. _____ |
| 6. | Is the assignment of work to employees a part of operations management? .... | yes no | 6. _____ |
| 7. | Will a group of employees usually have about the same level of motivation? .. | yes no | 7. _____ |
| 8. | Is self-actualization the lowest level on Maslow's Hierarchy of Needs? ........... | yes no | 8. _____ |
| 9. | Is McLelland's Achievement Motivation theory based on a belief that people are born with a common set of needs? ...................................................... | yes no | 9. _____ |
| 10. | Do the hygiene factors identified by Fredrick Herzberg provide dissatisfaction when they do not meet employee needs? ...................................................... | yes no | 10. _____ |
| 11. | In Herzberg's theory of motivation, do the same factors provide both satisfaction and dissatisfaction for people? ...................................................... | yes no | 11. _____ |
| 12. | Do people usually accept change easily? ...................................................... | yes no | 12. _____ |
| 13. | Is it usually best for managers to say nothing to employees about possible changes until a final decision has been made? ...................................................... | yes no | 13. _____ |
| 14. | Does effective change usually require that employees are provided information and training? ........................................................................................... | yes no | 14. _____ |
| 15. | Are there five basic steps in the controlling process? ..................................... | yes no | 15. _____ |
| 16. | Would the minimum number of units to be produced in a day be an example of a quantity standard? ........................................................................................ | yes no | 16. _____ |
| 17. | Is increasing sales the only way a business can increase its profits? ................. | yes no | 17. _____ |
| 18. | Is the difference between planned and actual performance known as profit? ... | yes no | 18. _____ |
| 19. | Should managers ever change the standard if a business is not meeting the standard that was set? ........................................................................................ | yes no | 19. _____ |
| 20. | Is safety training a way that companies can actually reduce costs? ................. | yes no | 20. _____ |

|  | Answers | For Scoring |
|---|---|---|

1. The set of factors that cause a person to act in a certain way is (a) management, (b) implementation, (c) control, (d) motivation. .......................... _____ 1. _____

2. A group of individuals who cooperate to achieve common goals is known as (a) supervisors, (b) an employee group, (c) a work teams, (d) motivators. ............ _____ 2. _____

3. The motivation theory based on five specific categories of need was developed by (a) Herzberg, (b) Maslow, (c) McClelland, (d) Taylor. .............................. _____ 3. _____

4. People who want to influence and control others have (a) an achievement need, (b) an affiliation need, (c) a power need, (d) all of the responses. .................... _____ 4. _____

5. Motivators are to hygiene factors as (a) Herzberg is to Maslow, (b) basic needs are to affiliation needs, (c) recognition is to achievement, (d) recognition is to working conditions. ...................... _____ 5. _____

6. Which of the following is an important step in effective change? (a) Move rapidly to implement the change. (b) Delay communications about the change until decisions have been made. (c) Involve the people affected in making decisions about the change. (d) Avoid offering too much support as people adjust to the change. ..................... _____ 6. _____

7. Which of the following is NOT a part of the controlling process? (a) establishing standards, (b) motivating employees, (c) measuring and comparing performance, (d) taking corrective action. ..................... _____ 7. _____

8. The value of a variance report to a manager is that (a) standards not being met are identified, (b) the amount of difference between a standard and actual performance can be determined, (c) time is saved that can be used to solve problems, (d) all of the responses. ..................... _____ 8. _____

9. A just-in-time control system would be most useful for managing (a) inventory, (b) credit, (c) theft, (d) none of the responses. ..................... _____ 9. _____

10. On average, the percentage of total sales lost each year by retailers to theft from customers and employees is (a) almost nothing, (b) 1-2%, (c) 6%, (d) 15%. .. _____ 10. _____

**Part C**—*Directions:* In the Answers column, write the letter of the word or expression in Column I that most closely matches each statement in Column II.

| Column I | Column II | Answers | For Scoring |
|---|---|---|---|
| A. Implementing | 1. Determining if goals are being met and actions needed if they are not. ................................. | _____ | 1. _____ |
| B. Controlling | 2. Two distinct groups of factors that contribute to employee satisfaction. ............................. | _____ | 2. _____ |
| C. Herzberg | 3. Power, affiliation, and achievement needs influence people's behavior. ............................. | _____ | 3. _____ |
| D. McClelland | 4. Carrying out plans and helping employees to work effectively. ......................................... | _____ | 4. _____ |
| E. Maslow | 5. People are motivated by five levels of needs beginning with physiological needs. ............. | _____ | 5. _____ |

**Directions:** Study each controversial issue carefully. Follow the advice of your teacher before listing in the columns provided reasons why people might answer Yes or No. Your teacher may want you to work with a classmate, talk with others in your community to gather information, or use the library to gather facts.

27-1. Even if a business is operating effectively and profitably, should the company's managers be planning for and implementing changes?

| Reasons for "Yes" | Reasons for "No" |
| --- | --- |
|  |  |

27-2. Do you agree with Herzberg's theory of motivation that pay, benefits, and working conditions can prevent employees from being dissatisfied or can actually dissatisfy employees but cannot provide satisfaction?

| Reasons for "Yes" | Reasons for "No" |
| --- | --- |
|  |  |

# PROBLEMS

**27-A.** Effective teams can make the difference in success or failure whether in a business, an athletic event, a class project, or in a club or other group. Using your own experience, identify one team or work group you have been a part of that you considered to be effective and one that you considered to be ineffective. Complete the following chart describing the characteristics of the team. Then answer the questions that follow the chart.

| | Effective Team | Ineffective Team |
|---|---|---|
| Characteristics | | |
| Description of the team | | |
| Purpose of the team | | |
| Did team members support the team's purpose? | | |
| Did each member understand his/her responsibilities? | | |
| Were all members committed to the group? | | |
| Were the activities to be completed clear? | | |
| Did members have the needed skills for success? | | |
| Did team members communicate effectively? | | |
| Did the team members work to solve problems? | | |

1. Did the characteristics of the team appear to affect whether the group was successful or not?

   _____

2. Which of the characteristics seemed to be most important to the group success?

   _____

3. Which of the characteristics seemed to contribute to group problems?

   _____

4. If you were helping to organize a new group or team, what would you do to try to make it more effective

   in achieving its goals? _____

**27-B.** Each of the following statements describes a principle of motivation. Read each statement and then select the theory that includes the principle by placing a check mark in the appropriate column.

| Principle of Motivation | Maslow | Herzberg | McClelland |
|---|---|---|---|
| 1. People satisfy security needs before social needs. | ___ | ___ | ___ |
| 2. The highest level of achievement is self-actualization. | ___ | ___ | ___ |
| 3. Needs can be developed that have a strong influence on people's behavior. | ___ | ___ | ___ |
| 4. Two distinct groups of factors contribute to employee satisfaction or dissatisfaction. | ___ | ___ | ___ |
| 5. A person with a power need wants to control and influence people. | ___ | ___ | ___ |
| 6. Until physiological needs are satisfied, people will be concerned about little else. | ___ | ___ | ___ |
| 7. Increases in pay will do little to motivate a worker. | ___ | ___ | ___ |
| 8. One group of workers will take personal responsibility for their work while another group will be more concerned about getting along. | ___ | ___ | ___ |
| 9. The greatest motivators are challenging work, recognition, and personal development. | ___ | ___ | ___ |

**27-C.** Hasme Manufacturing, Inc. produces small components for computer systems. Quality control is very important so each product is carefully tested when it is completed. If the product does not meet quality standards, it is rejected and returned for improvement. Management is also concerned that quantity standards are maintained so that orders are filled on schedule.

Jan Rankin, vice president of manufacturing, has collected information on production levels for four weeks. The production for each day of the week was totaled during the four-week period. The chart below shows the total number of items produced and the total number rejected for each day of the week for four weeks.

|  | Monday | Tuesday | Wednesday | Thursday | Friday |
|---|---|---|---|---|---|
| Total Parts Produced | 1,480 | 1,500 | 1,520 | 1,550 | 1,460 |
| Total Parts Rejected | 172 | 140 | 125 | 111 | 169 |

1. On which day of the week were the most acceptable components produced? _____

2. On which day were the fewest acceptable components produced? _____

3. How many parts were produced on an average work day at the Hasme Company? (Remember, information was collected for four weeks.) _____

4. How many parts were rejected on an average work day? _____

5. Using the information in the chart above, construct a bar graph on the form on the next page. The graph should show the percentage of component parts rejected for each day of the week.

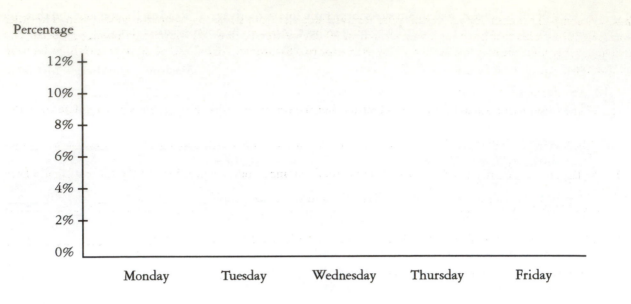

27-D. The following chart shows the projected and actual sales for several models of televisions in an appliance store. Complete the chart by calculating the amount the actual sales varied from the budgeted amounts. Next, calculate the percentage of variance for each item. Finally, determine the total variance between projected and actual sales and the percentage of variance between planned and actual sales.

| Model No. | Projected Sales | Actual Sales | Variance | Percentage Variance |
|---|---|---|---|---|
| XTL-13 | $ 11,325 | $ 13,250 | _____ | _____ |
| ZT-13 | 11,985 | 9,995 | _____ | _____ |
| XTL-15 | 12,840 | 10,620 | _____ | _____ |
| ZT-15 | 13,825 | 15,385 | _____ | _____ |
| MG-19 | 11,540 | 11,540 | _____ | _____ |
| RC-19 | 12,650 | 9,985 | _____ | _____ |
| MG-25 | 19,020 | 21,855 | _____ | _____ |
| RC-25 | 20,330 | 20,960 | _____ | _____ |
| MB-45 | 13,790 | 15,015 | _____ | _____ |
| Totals | _____ | _____ | _____ | _____ |

27-E. A company that manufactures bicycles received an order from a national sporting-goods chain. The order was for 150 bicycles that must be manufactured in 30 days. After 10 days, 45 bicycles had been produced. The manager scheduled the employees to work overtime for two Saturdays. At the end of 20 days, 110 bicycles were completed.

1. Write a standard for daily bicycle production that the company must meet in order to complete the order

    in the required 30 days. _____

2. At the end of the first ten days, what was the total variance from the number of bicycles that should have

    been completed? _____

3. What was the variance from the daily standard at the end of the first ten days? _____

4. What was the corrective action taken by the manager? _____

    _____

5. At the end of twenty days, what was the total variance from the number of bicycles that should have been

    completed? _____

6. Write a standard for the daily production of bicycles for the last ten days in order to complete the contract

    on schedule. _____

7. What should the manager do if the production level exceeds the standard during the first two of the

    remaining production days? _____

    _____

    _____

    _____

# CONTINUING PROJECT
## Chapter 27 Activities

If you hire employees to work for you, they must be motivated to work well. Managers must develop a theory of motivation and translate that into effective policies and procedures. The final step in business management is to determine if decisions are working well or if changes must be made. To do this you must establish standards, collect and study information, and take corrective action if needed. You will complete these activities in this chapter.

### Data Collection

1. Survey 10 people who are employed full- or part-time. Ask them to list the factors related to their work that motivate them to perform well and the factors that dissatisfy them. Using those factors, classify each person based on the motivation theories discussed in Chapter 27 that best describe their motivation.

2. Review sources of business information to identify industry performance standards that have been developed. Those standards can be quality, quantity, cost, or time. Determine how the standards were developed and how they are used by business managers.

### Analysis

1. Assume that you have several employees working for your business. Identify the factors you would use to motivate the employees to maintain effective performance. Estimate the cost of each of the motivation methods.

2. Develop a standard to evaluate each of the following activities in your business: (a) daily sales of each product, (b) amount of product spoilage and loss, and (c) customer satisfaction.